Born into Afghanistan during the wake of the Soviet Invasion, Laila narrowly escaped death and war. However, the harsh realities as a woman born into the culture of her homeland was something she was unable to escape wherever she had sought refuge. Laila had her innocence taken at a young age and was forced into an arranged and abusive marriage. She made the promise that when she wins her freedom, she'll do whatever had to be done to share her story.

In hopes to bring a voice to the silenced, *I Want Freedom* was penned to draw attention to the wrongdoing that can happen when a woman is pushed into situations over which she has no control.

To the women and young girls worldwide that are suffering from forced and abusive marriages. I hope my book inspires you to find the courage to fight for your freedom. Even though I may not know you, I feel you and I understand you.

Laila Eshan

I WANT FREEDOM

My Journey to Freedom

AUSTIN MACAULEY PUBLISHERS®

LONDON • CAMBRIDGE • NEW YORK • SHARJAH

Copyright © Laila Eshan 2024

All rights reserved. No part of this publication may be reproduced, distributed, or transmitted in any form or by any means, including photocopying, recording, or other electronic or mechanical methods, without the prior written permission of the publisher, except in the case of brief quotations embodied in critical reviews and certain other non-commercial uses permitted by copyright law. For permission requests, write to the publisher.

Any person who commits any unauthorized act in relation to this publication may be liable to criminal prosecution and civil claims for damages.

All of the events in this memoir are true to the best of author's memory. The views expressed in this memoir are solely those of the author.

Ordering Information
Quantity sales: Special discounts are available on quantity purchases by corporations, associations, and others. For details, contact the publisher at the address below.

Publisher's Cataloging-in-Publication data
Eshan, Laila
I Want Freedom

ISBN 9798891552739 (Paperback)
ISBN 9798891552746 (Hardback)
ISBN 9798891552760 (ePub e-book)
ISBN 9798891552753 (Audiobook)

Library of Congress Control Number: 2024905414

www.austinmacauley.com/us

First Published 2024
Austin Macauley Publishers LLC
40 Wall Street, 33rd Floor, Suite 3302
New York, NY 10005
USA

mail-usa@austinmacauley.com
+1 (646) 5125767

202241024

Table of Contents

Introduction

My name is Laila Eshan, and I survived an abusive arranged marriage. Against my will, I was married at age sixteen to a twenty-eight-year-old man who went on to abuse, control and repeatedly rape me over the course of our sixteen-year marriage. I'm sharing my story with you because, having finally found my freedom and independence, I believe I can offer my voice in service of all the young girls and women out there who are being forced into arranged marriages, or who are stuck in a cycle of abuse.

My ultimate goal is to change the dynamic of the culture and end this abusive custom of forced arranged marriages. My story, sadly, is far from unusual. The UN now regards what happened to me—which they refer to as "child and forced marriage"—as "a human rights violation and a harmful practice that disproportionately affects women and girls globally, preventing them from living their lives free from all forms of violence." Though progress has been made, today more than 650 million women alive were married as children; every minute, on average, 28 girls are forced into marriage[1].

In the country where I was born, Afghanistan, 33% of women are married before the age of 18[2]. Though these women's stories are diverse and unique, and I cannot speak for all of them, I hope that my story sheds light on the issue of child and forced marriage: why and how it happens, how it affects the women and families involved, and why it is so difficult to leave an abusive marriage.

I consider myself very lucky that, because I lived in the US, it was much easier for me to pull myself out of my forced arranged marriage than it would have been otherwise. Still, I was stuck for sixteen years—years of my life that I'll never get back. It's only by God's grace that I survived so much mental, physical and emotional abuse; not everyone is so lucky. Many women in situations like mine end up dying from suicide or being killed by their husbands. In many places, men can abuse and even kill their wives with impunity.

In Afghanistan, though legislation has been passed in the past decade to protect women and girls, these laws are

---

[1] My story, sadly, is far from unusual. The UN now regards what happened to me—which they refer to as "child and forced marriage"—as "a human rights violation and a harmful practice that disproportionately affects women and girls globally, preventing them from living their lives free from all forms of violence." Though progress has been made, today more than 650 million women alive were married as children; every minute, on average, 28 girls are forced into marriage.

[2] In the country where I was born, Afghanistan, 33% of women are married before the age of 18.

difficult to enforce, especially since the recent Taliban takeover. According to the Global Database of Violence Against Women, more than 50% of Afghan women have experienced intimate partner violence. For various reasons, many of these women effectively have no recourse[3].

This is a cultural problem with deep roots. In this book, I share my story from childhood to the present, beginning when Russia's invasion of Afghanistan split my family apart. I share all of this because I want my story to illuminate not only the problem of forced marriage itself but also how various forces result in girls and women being treated as second-class citizens. I want to make it clear how war, displacement, cultural traditions, and cycles of trauma within individual families all interact to create the situation I found myself in.

---

[3] I consider myself very lucky that, because I lived in the US, it was much easier for me to pull myself out of my forced arranged marriage than it would have been otherwise. Still, I was stuck for sixteen years—years of my life that I'll never get back. It's only by God's grace that I survived so much mental, physical and emotional abuse; not everyone is so lucky. Many women in situations like mine end up dying from suicide or being killed by their husbands. In many places, men can abuse and even kill their wives with impunity. In Afghanistan, though legislation has been passed in the past decade to protect women and girls, these laws are difficult to enforce, especially since the recent Taliban takeover. According to the Global Database of Violence Against Women, more than 50% of Afghan women have experienced intimate partner violence. For various reasons, many of these women effectively have no recourse.

I have long ago forgiven my family for putting me in this situation, as they were simply following tradition and likely assumed that they were somehow acting in my best interest as well as their own. But I cannot stand by while girls and women continue to suffer the same; the culture needs to change.

Now, I know the wonderful feeling of being my own person. I no longer belong to anyone. I no longer need to ask anyone what I'm allowed to do or not do. No more being insulted every day, no more pain, no more tears, no more ruined days, no more being forced to share my body. I can live my life just the way I want to: I can do whatever I want, go wherever I want, hang out with whomever I want. I'm no longer someone else's property; I'm safe, I'm independent, and I'm free. It took me a long time to learn how to be happy but today I'm the happiest woman, mother and a grandma. I want other women who've experienced the hopelessness of a forced marriage to know that this is possible for them too.

At the same time, it's also true that my scars—both physical and emotional—will be with me for the rest of my life. I suffer from various chronic health conditions that directly resulted from my abusive marriage. I and my children all suffer from adrenal gland insufficiency, a result of severe stress. I have facial palsy and nerve paralysis, likely an aftereffect of a broken jaw and other head injuries I endured at the hands of my husband. Other effects of the repeated head trauma include occipital neuralgia, memory loss, aneurysm and shattering headaches. Aside from physical symptoms, the emotional and psychological toll of my traumatic experiences will be with me for the rest of my life.

Writing my story was one of the most difficult things I've ever done. Revisiting each story I share in the subsequent pages was a stab of sorrows! Often, I couldn't hold back tears. Time and again, I questioned *how did this little girl survive, how was it possible?* Still, I knew that there were many stories out there even worse than mine. People told me, "Once you write and get it out, it'll get easier—it will heal you." That may be true to some extent, but I doubt that one can ever heal completely from an experience like this.

What gives me strength is the idea that my story might become meaningful by serving as a beacon of empathy and hope for others. I want to motivate and inspire women worldwide to be strong and brave, to believe in themselves, and to have faith. If you are in an abusive situation, know that there *is* a way out; there are brighter days ahead. If you stay focused, take care of your mind and body, and learn what resources are there to support you, things can still turn around for you. It's not too late. You are worth it. If you think we can help you, please don't hesitate to contact us through our website and tell us about your situation.

I also hope that this book raises awareness about this issue and inspires people who have not been directly affected by it to pitch in and help us make a change. If my story touches your heart and you are in a position to help, please consider donating to our non-profit foundation. Or if you think you can help in any way in this matter, please contact us through our website and let us know how you can help. Our mission is to help pull these young innocent girls and women out of their miserable lives and help them find safe homes and education. All proceeds of this book will be donated to this cause. Let's work together to free these innocent souls and change the culture of abuse.

1. https://en.wikipedia.org/wiki/Forced_marriage#cite_note-180
2. Iwantfreedom.ngo

Life Story

I remember the day like it was yesterday. It was fall of 1980 in Afghanistan; I was nine years old, playing hopscotch with my sister Sophia in front of our house. I couldn't possibly have known it at the time, but in many ways, this was the last moment of my childhood. Everything was about to change.

As the sun started to set, we suddenly heard a deafening noise. We thought it was fireworks, but as we looked up to search the sky, we heard our mother's voice screaming: "Get inside the house now! Those are not fireworks they're rockets!" We started running into the house, terrified; we had no idea what 'rockets' were.

Later, I overheard my mother talking to a neighbor, saying that our country was going to war with Russia. I didn't know exactly what that meant, but it sounded frightening. All my sister and I knew at that point was that something bad was about to happen.

After that day, the sound of fireworks became more frequent, and my parents began to argue about leaving the country. My father wanted to leave, explaining that his life was in danger because he worked for the Treasury Department; with the country at war, government officials were particularly at risk. But my mom would not go. She had no trust in my father: he had not only abused her physically but had also cheated on her and married another woman. If that wasn't enough, the passports he'd arranged for my mother and their five children said that we were his cousin and his cousin's children, while the second wife's passport acknowledged her as his wife. (At the time, women and children did not have their own passports, but were attached to the adult males.) This made my mother feel hurt and suspicious, and she refused to come along.

My father started making arrangements to move to Germany with his second wife. One day, I heard him telling my mother that he was planning to take my older sister with him. My mother immediately responded: "No! You can't take my girl away from me. I won't let that happen!"

My father yelled back, "I must take her! Living in Germany will help improve her asthma—besides that, it will be good for her future."

Hearing this, my stomach plummeted and my heart started to pound. The thought of my sister leaving was completely devastating. Sophia was my best friend, my playmate, and the one who always comforted me anytime my parents fought or yelled. Only eleven months older, she was like my twin, and we did everything together. I couldn't let her go without me.

The next day, I spoke with my father. I begged him to take me to Germany with my sister: "It's not fair! I want to go on a plane too." I cried and pleaded that I didn't want to be left behind. My dad just listened to me without saying a word. He seemed completely unaffected by my pleas, and I thought there was no hope.

A few days later, I overheard my mother telling someone that her husband wanted to take me with him to Germany. I was shocked and excited—until I heard her say, "There's no way in hell I would let him take my two oldest kids away from me. I won't allow it."

When I went to my mother and begged her to let me go, she cried and told me that there was no way. But I insisted; as scared as I was of her, I didn't back down. I needed her to understand how badly I wanted to go with my sister.

My parents continued to argue about this for quite some time. Seeing and hearing them fight over me made me very anxious and scared. I was so young, and all I wanted was to go on the plane ride and be with my sister wherever she went.

Soon after that, my uncle came to our house with my grandmother. My mother told us to stay in the yard while she talked to them. I had no idea what that visit was about, but my uncle and grandmother had never visited us before, so it had to be something serious. As they were leaving, I saw that my mom's eyes were red and watery; she had been crying. That's when I knew the visit was about my departure to Germany. I could see that my mom felt extremely upset and helpless, but all I could think about was the journey I would soon make with my sister.

Before I knew it, I was at my grandmother's house. It was March 16, 1980, the day before our flight, and we were packed and ready to go. I remember saying goodbye to my grandpa, who was the most loving and caring person in my life. As he hugged me goodbye, he started to cry. I couldn't figure out why he was crying. Four years later, when I received news of his death, I thought of that moment and realized he'd been crying because he had known he might never see me again.

Along with our father, stepmother and one-year-old half-sister, Sophia and I finally boarded our plane at the airport in Kabul, wearing matching brown corduroy suits that my mom had had a tailor make for us, with our long hair hanging down our backs. It was amazing being in a new environment and meeting so many new people. Everyone treated us with kindness. We made good friends with the flight attendants, who took us to the front of the plane to meet the pilots. The cockpit looked like a big toy to us, with so many different buttons. It was our first glimpse of the new world we were being introduced to.

When we arrived in Frankfurt, we were shepherded into a crowded room with other refugees. My sister and I were clueless as to what was going on. The immigration officer finally called us into a small office, and began interrogating my dad. They asked my father many questions, and then finally let us go.

The next thing I remember is being in a hotel, where I began to fall asleep on the couch. Surrounded by strangers, I saw my dad sitting across the room. He came to me and said, "Let me carry you to bed. Let's get you in the other room."

My stepmom looked at my father carrying me and said, "Why do you have to carry her? Why don't you let her walk to bed?"

I thought to myself, *why wouldn't she want dad to carry me? I'm so tired, I just want to be carried.* I suddenly missed my mom and wanted to go back. I felt scared and lonely, wishing for the comforts of my own home.

Our hotel was large, seven stories tall; we had two rooms on the top floor. My dad and his wife had one room with our half-sister, and my sister and I had the other room. Our room was also the kitchen/living room; there were two twin size beds, a small portable stove on top of a little table with a tiny sink next to it, and a mini-refrigerator.

On one of our first days there, my stepmom was cooking lunch while Sophia and I played with a small ball that someone had gifted us. That ball was the first toy we'd ever had in our lives, and it was so fun and exciting to play with. Unfortunately, my stepmom was bothered by our playing. She asked us to stop, but we were having too much fun to listen. That made her upset; she took the ball away from us and made us leave the room. We both got very scared and didn't know where to go. We wandered the halls and finally sat in the hallway on the stairs. We looked at each other and started to cry. We longed for our mom more than ever.

We knew then that it wasn't going to be easy living with our stepmom. It was very obvious that she didn't care for us. The only time she talked to us was when she wanted us to do chores around the hotel: cleaning, doing dishes, laundry, grocery shopping or taking care of her daughter, Adia. It became obvious that we meant little more to her than a source of free labor. We had no idea this was what we were getting ourselves into when we left home. While our mom had made us do the same kind of chores, she also cared about us and frequently demonstrated her love. She would often get mad at us and hit us for making mistakes, but she would always eventually calm down and hold us and cry, saying how sorry she was for hitting us. She would explain to us that she didn't mean to be this way, but that it was hard for her to manage because our father was never around, and when he was, he was mean and abusive.

After that day in the hotel, we would fall asleep crying every single night, missing our mom and talking about how much we wanted to go back. But we knew that idea was out of the question. Our dad was trying to get us to call our stepmother 'Mom', which didn't make any sense: she wasn't our mother. We asked if we could call her Mother Sima since she wasn't our real mother, but she refused. She said, "No need to add my name. Just simply call me Mom." This left us with no choice.

I was my stepmom's favorite out of the two of us, because I always ignored it when she talked negatively or disrespectfully about my biological mother. Perhaps because Sophia was older, it affected her more. But I felt that it didn't make sense for me to react; I would get better results by trying to endear myself to my stepmom, rather than resisting her at every turn. I became her wardrobe coordinator, her nail manicurist, her make-up artist and her hairstylist. She wouldn't go shopping without me. She made my sister do more chores, and she made it obvious that she didn't like her very much.

When we'd been in Germany for a few months, Sophia told me that there were rumors going around that we had both started our periods.

I asked, "What's a period?"

She replied, "I think it's when you see blood in your underwear."

I didn't know what she meant by that. "How do you get that?"

She turned to me with teary eyes and said, "I really don't know."

June 1980 with my sisters, Sophia and Adia, by the Frankfurt main river

I started to panic and thought, *Oh gosh, I'm in trouble again.* I asked, "Where did you hear that from?"

She said, "One of our stepmom's friends, Auntie Fausya." Auntie Fausya was also my dad's cousin. I felt relieved hearing this; I thought that, if anything, she would be on our side. Out of all their friends, she was the nicest to us. At the same time, I felt lost, confused, and scared. I didn't know what to do. The only thing I knew was that the rumor wasn't true: I had never seen blood in my underwear.

So many questions pounded through my head: *Why would I get blood in my underwear? Is that something bad? Would people gossip about us now? What would happen to us once this rumor got to my father? Would he hit us? Why would my stepmom spread this kind of rumor in the first place?* I had no idea what to do next.

After a while, I went to our room and found our stepmom cooking. She asked me to help her. As we worked, she looked down at me and simply said: "*I know.*"

"What do you mean, you know?"

She said, "Don't worry about it. I just want you to know that I know."

I wanted to cry so badly, but I held my tears. I told her, "I have no idea what you're talking about."

She said, "Really? You have no idea?"

"No, I don't."

She turned to me and said, "Okay, once I'm done cooking, I'm going to check you."

At that moment, my heart started to race, and I wanted to be anywhere but there. I thought to myself, *there is no way I can let her see my naked body.*

I had no idea how to solve the problem. I had never seen blood in my underwear, but I had noticed that I'd recently begun growing a couple of hairs on my private parts. As soon as I got done helping my stepmom in the kitchen, I ran to the bathroom as fast as I could, locked myself in, and took off my bottoms. I stood there crying, trying to figure out how to get rid of the hairs. First, I grabbed a pair of scissors. My hands started to shake. I thought to myself, *what if I cut my skin by accident? Then she'll see blood in my underwear—that's not gonna be good.* Then I grabbed my dad's razor, and thought of shaving the hairs. But I remembered that when my dad shaved his face, I still saw hair under his skin.

So, there I was, standing in the bathroom with my pants down, hysterically crying, thinking of my mom and yearning to be back home with her. Finally, I decided to shave the hairs and take my chances. Whatever happened would happen. I was beyond relieved to find that the hair under my skin wasn't visible. I was now ready for my stepmom to check me—but after all that, she never did. I felt relief, but at the same time I resented her. I couldn't stand her after that.

Within the next couple of days, Aunt Fausya approached us and asked us if we had started our periods. Scared and confused, we responded defensively, telling her that we weren't sure what a period was. She sat us down and explained what it meant. We told her that the rumor wasn't true: we had never experienced anything like that. She clearly believed us, and we exhaled a long sigh of relief. We were so happy that we no longer had to deal with this.

As time went by, almost every day there was something we did or said that set off our stepmom's anger. We were just two sad little girls missing our mom, and we never knew why we were getting in trouble. We waited every day for bedtime, which was the most exciting part of our day because then we could share our feelings about our daily experiences. Our stepmom's behavior never made sense to us, and even our dad seemed so different compared to how he was in Afghanistan. In Afghanistan, we'd hardly seen him: after he got married to his second wife, he made a deal with my mom to take turns coming to stay with us every other night. In the little time we did spend with him, he had been much nicer than he was now.

One day, I was sitting in our room doing my homework at the dining table. I heard my stepmom screaming to me, "Hurry, take the knife from Adia! Hurry!" As I looked up, I saw my younger half-sister standing between her mother and I, holding a big butcher's knife. I was so scared that I sprang into action; without thinking twice, I got up from my chair. She started to run; I chased her. Finally, I was able to grab the knife from her, but she tried to pull it back. As a result, the knife sliced two inches off the back of my left hand. The cut went all the way down to the bone.

I was in shock, unsure of what was happening. The wound didn't bleed right away. All I could see was something very white, but I wasn't sure what it was. Soon I realized it was my bone. My hand started to bleed very heavily, accompanied by an excruciating burning pain. I had no idea what to do. I turned to my stepmom with my bleeding hand, but she didn't say anything.

I told her, "She cut me!"

She just replied, "Cover it with some paper—it'll be fine."

Hours later, my hand was still bleeding, and I was feeling very weak. My dad and stepmom had guests over; as they walked in, someone asked me what was wrong. It must have been obvious that I was hurt. My dad spoke for me, saying, "Her baby sister cut her hand when she was trying to take the knife away from her."

The guest—a man we called 'uncle', though he wasn't a blood relative—took a look at my hand and said, "This cut is pretty deep. You can see to her bone. She needs to go to the hospital and will most likely need stitches."

When my father heard this, he looked to my sister, who was setting the table for dinner. He said, "Take your sister to the hospital. Your uncle says she may need some stitches on her cut."

So, there we were, ages nine and ten, walking through the dark cold streets to try and find the hospital. We had no idea where it was; we had no choice but to stop people on the street and ask directions with our broken German. Finally, after over an hour, we found it. When we walked in, the first thing the hospital staff asked us was where our parents were.

My sister Sophia replied, "Our parents sent us on our own. They wanted us to tell you that my sister's hand needs stitches."

The nurse looked stunned at the sight of us, but she was very kind. She sat us in a room with all kinds of different people who had come to the hospital for different reasons. We had never seen an emergency room before, and the environment was so new and different that I became absorbed in my surroundings and almost forgot about my pain.

After the doctor examined me, he said, "Yes, we do need to stitch you up. But first, if you would like to call your parents, you can."

I said, "They can't come, they have guests over."

The doctor looked at us, astonished. It was clear that he and the other hospital staff pitied us. I remember feeling embarrassed, like we were not important enough for our dad to be there with us. I told myself, *I am obviously less important than their guests, people I don't even know and have never seen before—but I can't change the situation, I'll just have to deal with it.* I felt angry and sad to have been put in that position; though I didn't expect much from my father at this point, I instinctively knew that I deserved better care. The hospital staff's reaction only seemed to confirm this.

September 1983, me in the backyard

As our new life continued, our chores became harder and harder. My stepmom was very particular about how she wanted things done around the house. She divided the house chores between us, according to a strict schedule. One day, everything would be my full responsibility, and the next day my sister's. The hardest chores for us to do were the laundry, ironing and grocery shopping. We had a brutal 40-minute walk home from the grocery store, carrying heavy bags. Back then, in Germany, there were no dryers in a typical home. All the small items—such as underwear, socks and baby stuff—we had to hand-wash. We hung large items like sheets and big towels, and ironed them as well. We ironed all clothes except socks.

At first, we were doing five people's laundry and grocery shopping, but soon the number grew to seven—during our first three years in Germany, my stepmom had two more babies. She had my sister Nadia first, and then three years later, my brother Sal. As the family grew, our responsibilities grew. We had to take care of the babies from the time they were newborns. We were like housewives; we did more parenting of those three children than their parents did, from handling all of their immunization shots and doctor's appointments to giving them baths and changing diapers.

When the kids started going to grade school, we were responsible for fixing their lunch boxes, waking them up, and getting them dressed. It was our job to keep them quiet so they wouldn't wake our parents up. Then, though my dad had a car and could have driven them, we would walk them to their school, which was in the opposite direction from our school. This doubled our walk from 20 minutes to 45 minutes—longer if they asked us to carry them. The winters in Germany were bitterly cold, the temperature sometimes dipping below zero; by the time we got to our school, our eyes and noses were so frozen that we couldn't blink. It was quite hard and challenging for us.

The rumors about us starting our period never stopped; every so often they would surface again, but we just tried to ignore them. I actually started my period at the age of thirteen and a half; by now, we had relocated to a tall apartment building where some of my parents' friends that had kids our age also lived. One evening we were all at one of our friends' apartments, watching a movie on TV with our parents. I felt something warm in my panties; when I went to the bathroom, I noticed blood on my underwear.

By now, I knew what it was. I wasn't sure what to do— no one had explained to me how to use period products. I just washed off and changed my panties, but soon found them dirtied again. I realized that a period wasn't a one-time thing and that it lasted for a while—maybe I should use some toilet paper to absorb the blood? When I realized toilet paper wasn't going to be enough, I started to wear paper towels. I did this for a long time, at least until I got married. I always thought getting your period was a bad thing and could get me in trouble; I was very embarrassed about it and hid it from everyone except my sister.

When I was graduating from ninth grade and my sister from tenth, there was a celebration party at school, during which we'd collect our diplomas. My sister and I were very excited about this, for weeks leading up to it. It was our first school event that we assumed we would be allowed to go to. We had already planned what to wear, although we didn't have a lot of clothes.

We told our parents about our graduation a couple of times per week prior to the day. They always stayed quiet, so we assumed they had no objection. But finally, our stepmom told us we couldn't go. We pleaded, but no matter what we said, she said no. We couldn't believe that she wouldn't let us go; her reason was, "I never attended events like that—I don't see why you guys should get to go."

None of it made any sense to us. My sister and I were going back and forth to our dad and asking him for his response. But he just said, "If your mom is okay with it, then go; otherwise, it's best you guys stay put."

We were both crushed. We had been so excited about this one event, and now, at the very last minute, we couldn't go. I finally went to my dad and cried my heart out to him. I said, "This isn't about us going to a party. This is an event for all students that are finishing their grade and collecting our diplomas. That's all there is."

He finally said, "Let me talk to your mom." He then came back and said, "Okay, let's get ready and I'll drop you guys off, just so you can get your diplomas. But you can't stay. I'll be waiting in my car and will expect you back in fifteen minutes."

Our hearts were full of sadness. We didn't understand why exactly we weren't allowed to attend our celebration, but we figured anything was better than not going at all. We skipped our showers, quickly put on our outfits, and went to the school. Some of our friends were happy to see us, but sadly, by the time we greeted everyone, it was already time to leave.

Our teachers told us they had already passed out the diplomas and we could just pick ours up from the school's office.

The day that changed everything for us came when I was sixteen years old.

As our house chores and responsibilities increased, so had our schoolwork; I was busily studying for final exams at my desk when my younger half-sister Adia walked in my room.

She said, "Mom needs you to iron the clothes."

"I'm studying," I replied.

She left the room, came back and said it again: "Mom wants you to iron the laundry."

"I can't," I said. "I really have to study."

She came in one last time and made the request again. This made no sense to me: why did she keep asking? I told her, "It's not even my turn. It's Sophia's turn."

Once she left the room, I heard my stepmom walk out of her bedroom and stood in front of our dining table. This was about twenty feet away from my bedroom. My door was open, because we were never allowed to close our doors. "Why are you not ironing the clothes?" she hissed.

I told her, "I'm sorry, I can't. I have to study for finals."

She accused me of lying, saying that Adia had told her I was drawing hearts rather than studying. I was furious. "If you don't believe me, just come and look at my papers!" I spoke.

This made my stepmom very upset. She picked up a small cowboy boot made out of clay—we used it to hold toothpicks—and threw it at me.

The object hit the side of my hipbone with a force that took my breath away. I instantly fell out of my chair and crumpled into a tiny ball on the floor. My hip hurt so much I couldn't breathe. It felt hot and painful, as though she had shattered my bone. I struggled to digest the pain. It was worse than the cut on my hand, much worse than the few times I had broken bones.

My stepmom made no effort to help me. Instead, she turned and yelled at my dad: "I'm going to take our kids and go for a walk. By the time I get back, I want you to make a decision. It's either us or them." I knew she meant my sister and I.

As I lay on the floor, I listened carefully for my father's response, but I only heard silence. Apparently, he wasn't going to speak up for us. This put a fire in me that burned. We'd put up with a lot, but this was too much.

I lay there waiting for the awful pain to subside. Finally, I heard the front door slam shut, and I knew that my stepmom had left.

While all of this was happening, my sister was at her first job, at the Wendy's in the Frankfurt train station. She had only been working there a week. I told myself, *swallow the pain and get up. You have to get out of here and find your sister.* I struggled to my feet and managed to grab our school bags and toothbrushes. I quietly shut my bedroom door and opened the blinds. We were living in a single-story house at this point. I saw my stepmom outside, pushing the stroller. I laughed a little; it was funny because I'd never seen her pushing a stroller before. That was our job.

I waited for her to get a little further away from the house, until I could no longer see her. Then I jumped out of my bedroom window with both our backpacks and started to run as fast as I could. For a moment I forgot about my pain. It was still there, but I couldn't afford to acknowledge it. My goal was to get to the payphone before my sister got off work. I didn't want to miss her, so I ran as fast as I could. Finally, I reached the payphone and called her.

To my relief, she picked up. Trying to catch my breath, I panted into the phone: "Stay where you are. *Do not come home!* I'll come to you and I will tell you everything." I hung up the phone and ran toward the train station.

I had no money, so I got on a train with no ticket. Sometimes, if you were lucky, you could get away with having no ticket, but other times you'd get caught before even reaching the first stop. I felt sweaty and numb, my heart racing in my chest: *What if I get caught? What if I go to jail? And on top of it all, I ran away from home, and I can't go back.* Every time someone got up, I thought they were the conductor. I prayed to God to just get me to my sister's workplace. Fortunately, He answered my prayers. I was so relieved when the train pulled into the station: I'd made it.

I noticed my sister from a distance, sitting with her elbows on a table outside Wendy's, her hands resting on her cheeks. I tried to wave at her, but she didn't see me. Once I started walking closer, she immediately got up and noticed how hard I was breathing. She grabbed her backpack from me and asked, "What happened?"

Before I was able to answer her, I started to cry. I couldn't stop. She tried to calm me down, but that only made it worse. When I finally got myself to stop, I told her everything.

She wanted to see where my stepmother had hit me. I was too scared to show it to her. I hadn't even looked at the injury myself.

I told her, "I can't. It's too painful to even think about." But somehow, she convinced me. With her help, we managed to pull a couple inches of my pants down. My hip was black and blue, with a lump swollen to the size of a tennis ball. Just looking at it made us both cry.

She asked me, "Are you still in pain?" I told her I wasn't because I didn't want her to worry about me. I figured that since I wasn't bleeding, I would be okay.

Now that I had finished telling her everything, we had no idea what to do next. We put our heads together and tried to think of someone to call, someone who we could trust. It wasn't easy because everyone we knew, we knew through our parents. We weren't allowed to have any friends of our own.

We then remembered a couple who we called Uncle Abdul and Aunt Johanna. Uncle Abdul was my dad's cousin who was in his late thirties; his wife Johanna was in her early thirties. She was from Holland, and they had no children. They lived in Bonn, which was about a four-hour drive away. We both remembered them being very loving toward us; every time they came to visit, they would bring us games, chocolate, coloring books and all kinds of kids' stuff. We knew they were nice to us because they felt badly for us. Whenever they came down, they would stay the full weekend, and they noticed us spending most of our time in the kitchen or taking care of our three little siblings.

We felt good about our decision to call Uncle Abdul and Aunt Johanna. When we called, Uncle Abdul answered the phone. We were silent for a second. Then we both started to talk at the same time, saying, "Hi Uncle! We called you because we think we can trust you. Can you please tell us if we can trust you?"

He said, "Of course, honey, of course you can trust me."

"Okay…but promise us that you will not tell anyone what we are about to tell you."

"Okay, I promise."

We felt reassured; the tone of his voice was calm, yet concerned. He said, "You two need to know that your aunt Johanna and I are here for you, whatever you need."

When he said that, I told him the whole story, through my tears. He asked me where we were and told us to stay there.

We waited for four hours. We were both tired and hungry. The smell of all the fast food around us wasn't making it any easier. We held our stomachs to try to shut down the rumbling and ease the hunger pains. Eventually, I somehow fell asleep on the bench.

When I woke up, my mouth was so dry I couldn't open it. My lips were glued to each other; I had to use my fingers to open them. I knew I was thirsty; I knew I had cried a lot, and I knew I needed to drink water.

As I was looking for a water fountain, I noticed my uncle looking for us. I started to yell at my sister, "Grab our backpacks! They're here!"

We were so happy to see them. The first thing they asked was whether we were hungry. We were too shy and embarrassed to say yes, but it must have been obvious that we were starving. They told us, "No worries. We brought you two some snacks. When we get in the car, you can eat." For the first time in years, we felt real love and care. We couldn't believe that they had not only gone out of their way to drive four hours to get us, but they'd also taken the time to pack us food. It felt so wonderful, like being wrapped in a warm blanket. In the car, we talked for a little while; the next thing I knew, I heard a voice telling me, "Honey, wake up, we are home." We went straight to their guest room and fell asleep instantly.

The next day, we woke up to a table full of all kinds of yummy breakfast food. There were breakfast rolls with butter, Nutella and jelly; salami, boiled eggs, and over five different types of cheese; and orange juice and milk to drink. It felt amazing to just sit and eat without having to worry about chores. During breakfast, they told us that they were going to take us to their local schools to enroll us, but when we got to the schools, the staff refused. They said that since we were underage, we needed our parents' signature. In other words, our aunt and uncle would need to legally adopt us in order for the school to accept us as students. We tried a few other schools, but they all said the same thing.

After two weeks of trying, we were forced to go back to our original school. We knew the absence had made our grades suffer, which was devastating. We were both so determined, and had big dreams of becoming successful. We wanted to make a lot of money so we could help get our mom and three siblings out of Afghanistan, and then live together in a big house of our own.

Unfortunately, our aunt and uncle had to bring us back to Frankfurt. That was a very sad day for all of us. I remember Aunt Johanna crying a lot, apologizing again and again for not being able to help us more. They decided to drop us off at our caseworker's office (we'd been assigned a caseworker since we were refugees). Aunt Johanna and Uncle Abdul told us over and over what to say to the caseworker, and helped us rehearse. They told us to be honest about our challenges at home, so she'd feel badly for us and want to help us. It was the caseworker's job to help us find a safe home.

We talked to the caseworker for over three hours, telling her everything. She listened quietly, and then told us to wait in her office. She left for a few minutes; when she came back, she apologized and said that due to our ages, there was nothing she could do. We looked at each other, stunned. We knew that our situation was now more hopeless than ever.

We grabbed our backpacks with our heads down and left her office. As soon as we walked out of the building, we saw a tall skinny man walking toward us. As we got closer to him, he began to look familiar, and we realized that he was our dad. That's when we knew exactly what the social worker had done when she left her office: she had called him.

Our hearts sank—but what happened next surprised us. As soon as we got face-to-face with him, our father started to sob. He got down on his knees and begged us to come home, promising us that from now on things at home would be different. He promised that we'd have fewer chores so that we could have more time to study. He promised that there would be no more accusations and that our stepmom wouldn't talk badly about our mother anymore. He claimed that he'd realized all his mistakes and he didn't want to punish us for running away.

My sister and I could not believe what he was saying or how he was acting. We were so shocked that we started to cry with him. We told him, "Dad, please stop crying. Stand up! We don't want to see you down on your knees like this. If you promise things are going to be better at home, then we'll come back."

He looked at us and replied, "Whatever you want." So, we trusted him and went back home with him.

My father's remorse may well have been sincere, and indeed, when we got home, the atmosphere seemed to have shifted. Our stepmother gave us a break from chores and her attitude toward us was less punitive. But, as it turned out, this new peace would last only a few days before we encountered an entirely new set of problems. My father had had an ulterior motive for getting us home: plans were brewing to marry both of us off.

I had already started to receive proposals. I was very pretty and had grown into the perfect housewife: my stepmom had given me plenty of practice with housework, and I took cooking class as an elective in school. I had my first proposal at the age of thirteen, and received five in total before I was married off.

Customarily, proposals had to go through a male relative; in my case, they often came through an uncle of mine. This uncle was a real big-shot; back before Russia invaded Afghanistan, he had been the district attorney of Kabul. He'd studied politics abroad in France. He was also a ring fighter, an author, and was very athletic, tall, and handsome. He had settled in Paris after the war started, but he would often come and live with us for months at a time. He held Godlike stature in our family, and no one would dare to contradict him.

Whenever people approached my uncle to ask for my hand, he told them I was already spoken for and that I needed to finish school. Since I was six months old, there had been a plan in place that I would marry my first cousin in Afghanistan and my uncle wasn't interested in other offers for me.

He blamed me for attracting these proposals; he believed that I was more focused on my looks than on my schoolwork, that I only cared about fashion, and that my behavior was to blame for the male attention that came my way. His evidence consisted of the fact that I liked to shower and to wear different clothes every day. I liked to be clean, and it was too boring for me to repeat the same outfit for days in a row; I was interested in fashion and enjoyed putting a good look together. I never understood why any of this was a problem, since I always completed my schoolwork and got good grades.

But in my uncle's eyes, I was trouble. Many times, when he was staying with us, he would punish me for these supposed offenses by slapping me and beating me with the buckle part of his belt until my back would bleed.

Sometimes when I didn't get my Quran reading right, he would put pencils between my fingers and squeeze them as hard as he could. I was too prideful to show him that he was hurting me, but inside it felt like my heart was about to burst. Every time he squeezed, I would inhale the pain, then hold my breath and freeze.

I never directly contradicted him, but out of anger and pride, I continued to do what I wanted to do, since I couldn't stop him from beating me anyway. Till this day, I wonder how someone could be that highly educated, speak multiple languages, and yet beat the crap out of a little girl. As for me, I was still too young to be truly interested in marriage, but I did like someone. Zabi was a boy whose parents were close friends with mine. Our families often got together on the weekend. Zabi used to sing and play accordion; my parents enjoyed his music very much. I started to develop an innocent crush on him (he was three years older than me). Somehow my sister told him that I liked him, and he shared with her that he liked me back. He mentioned that his parents were waiting for me to get a little older, and then ask my parents for my hand.

But that wasn't to be, as I'd soon find out. Despite my uncle's plans for me, or my own dreams for myself, my parents made other arrangements for my marriage.

Uncle Azim, my stepmom's brother-in-law, used to come and visit us almost every summer, and he would always call me his 'pretty daughter-in-law'. At the beginning, I didn't take him seriously, but as time went on, it started to feel like a distinct possibility. I knew that my stepmom was interested in setting me up with Uncle Azim's son, Omar.

Two years earlier, in the summer of 1984, my father had sent my sister Sophia and I to Los Angeles, California, for two weeks. We had stayed with Uncle Azim and his family. I was fourteen years old at the time. One day, during our stay, Omar took a day off work to take my sister and I to Laguna Beach. We did some swimming and sightseeing, and he got us a banana split. As we were walking and talking on the beach, he suddenly asked, "What do you think about marrying me?"

The question stunned me. I was a very shy girl; I often felt embarrassed and awkward. I had no idea how to tell him that I was not interested in marriage at such a young age. I didn't know how to say that I just wanted to finish school and become successful so I could support my family from Afghanistan. I wanted to be the first Afghan female pilot; I wanted to be the next Sophia Loren; I wanted to become an important and famous person so I could help all the people I'd left behind. Within our culture, it would have been inappropriate for me to say such things, even though I'd been raised in Germany.

After hesitating, I eventually said, "It's not in my control. From what I know, it's my father's decision." I was hoping to just leave it at that and get the conversation over with.

In the summer of 1985, my stepmom went to the US to visit her family. One night, my sister and I were sitting with my dad in our living room and he called my stepmom in the US to see how she was doing. I could easily overhear everything they were saying. There was a lot of background noise; my father asked, "What's going on? Are you at a party or something?"

My stepmom replied, "No, I am at my sister's house. Just so you know, I gave Laila's sweets!"

I was shocked. This was a colloquial expression meaning that she'd accepted a proposal for my hand. Despite all of the previous talk about setting me up with Omar, I was shocked that she had gone and done it. I remember my father saying, "What did you do? Why didn't we discuss this before?" I couldn't hear her reply.

When she returned, she brought me a sapphire ring with little diamonds around it, along with some new outfits. She told me the ring was my engagement ring. I never wore the ring or the outfits—they all looked like an old lady's stuff to me.

I told Zabi that my stepmom had gotten me engaged with her nephew. Neither of us were particularly surprised, but Zabi told me he would ask his parents to come ask for my hand. A couple of months later, when they came to ask, my father took great offense at their proposal. He used an Afghan expression: "You come to my house, drink my water and eat my salt, then you pee on my name!"

After that, his parents stopped being friends with my parents for many years. No matter how many times Zabi's older brothers called my dad and stepmom, explaining that Zabi and I liked each other, my father told them, "I don't want people to think that my friendship with you guys was so I could sell my daughter to you just because you are rich." (Zabi's family owned a few fine jewelry stores in Edaroberstein, four hours' drive from Frankfurt.)

I knew that it was only a matter of time before the topic of my marriage would come up again. But I didn't think it would be so soon.

One day, less than two weeks after my sister and I had returned from running away, I came home from school; my stepmom asked me to make some tea and serve it to our guests in the living room. She wouldn't tell me who they were. She simply said it was a surprise.

When I walked in, carrying the tea tray, I suddenly saw Uncle Azim and Omar. I was devastated. I knew exactly why they were visiting us all the way from America: they were here to follow through on the marriage proposal. At that moment I just wanted to disappear.

Standing in front of them, I started to shake. I had no idea how to greet them, knowing that they were there to take me away from my sister and my hopes for the future. If I was married off, all of those dreams would fade like a mirage.

I set the tray on the table and greeted them very awkwardly. After serving them their tea, I went straight to my room, shut the door, and started to cry. I remember looking up and asking God: *Please help me, bring my mom so maybe she can save me.* I knew I was in over my head, that the situation was beyond my control. I felt sick to my stomach. I knew I wasn't ready to become a wife (and soon, inevitably, a mother). Why would my father want to do this to me?

After we'd returned home, my father had promised my sister and I that we could do whatever we wanted so we would come back home with him. I'd believed him at the time, but now I knew that he had lied to us—only to bring me home so he could marry me off to some stranger, a person I'd met only once. I didn't like Omar or think anything of him, except for the fact that he looked as old as my dad (in reality, he was twenty-eight at the time, but to a sixteen-year-old girl, he might have been fifty). I had so many questions, but sadly, I knew I couldn't ask them. If I did, I would get beaten and most likely sent to the United States even sooner.

Shortly after the meeting, my sister Sophia knocked on my door. I opened the door with a burst of tears. I told her, "They're going to marry me off and send me far away. I don't want to marry him! I'm not ready!"

As soon as she saw me, she started to cry with me. She held me tight, trying to comfort me. She wiped my tears and said, "You remember how you always said you want to be the next Sophia Loren? Well, this is your chance! You can't be a pilot anymore, but you can be a movie star because you're going to America! Isn't that what you always wanted to do too?"

I looked at her and said, "Yes, I do, but not now. I just don't want to get married right now. I'm not ready to be touched by a man and to have to sleep with him." It was all happening so suddenly.

When I woke up the next day, everyone was gone. Hours later, they came back with shopping bags and told me that they'd found a place for my wedding. My stepmom started to tell me that I had to go with them tomorrow to get fitted for a green dress for my Nikah. (Nikah is the religious ceremony required by Islamic law to unite a Muslim man and woman in holy matrimony.)

I asked, "Why green?"

She explained, "When we go to the mosque for the Nikah, the bride must be in a green dress with a green scarf to cover her head."

The next day, we went shopping for a green dress. I went through the motions numbly, following my stepmom's instructions because I had no idea how to resist. I was very small, so it was hard to find a ladylike dress that fit my body. We finally found one, but the waist still needed to be taken in. The tailor was shocked: she told me that in her thirty years of tailoring, she had never met anyone with a waist size of eighteen inches. That's why I always thought I could be a movie star like Sophia Loren and Elizabeth Taylor, who had tiny waists (I had no idea they were wearing girdles).

Now that we'd gotten the dress, we needed to find the matching head scarf. Even though I barely had any clothes, I loved fashion and knew a lot about it. I wanted my scarf to be the same exact color as my dress. To me that was the most important rule of fashion: things needed to match. Unfortunately, I was forced to get one that was a much different shade. The dress was forest green, but my scarf was neon green; they clashed horribly, and I hated the combination. No matter what I told stepmom, she didn't care; the scarf was cheap, and she wanted me to make it work.

The whole drive home, I thought about what I could do to change the color of my scarf. As soon as we got home, I told everyone I wanted to pop out to the store to get some cake mix so that I could make some cake for the afternoon tea. Really, I had another motivation: I thought I would get some food coloring and color the scarf. But when I got to the store, the ladies there told me that wouldn't work. I felt angry and helpless; I was going to change the color of my scarf one way or another. There was so little about the situation that I could control: I needed to have just this one thing the way I wanted it.

It was Sunday, so most of the stores were closed, but after walking for over an hour, I finally came across a paint shop. I walked in and found the exact color I was looking for, but the store owner told me that wall paint wouldn't work. I didn't listen, telling myself I'd make it work somehow. I bought the paint.

Back home, determined, I soaked the mesh scarf in a tub of water, threw some wall paint in and let it soak. Then I left it out on the balcony to dry. Initially, it seemed like my plan had worked…until the scarf dried out. It was the perfect color, but once I touched it, it felt hard and brittle, like foil. The surface cracked in little pieces and the green paint flaked off. Standing there on the balcony, holding the ruined scarf, I didn't know how to contain my disappointment.

Suddenly, Omar appeared behind me. "How are you doing?"

Every time he tried to talk to me, I did my best to avoid him. I would get very shy and embarrassed, unable to even look him in the eye. I started to reply in a whisper. He asked me to speak up.

I told him, "I'm not really ready to get married, but I understand that I have no right to say no. I just have a favor to ask of you—can you promise me something?"

He said, "Sure. Anything."

It was very hard for me to even bring it up, but I knew I had to. I told him, "I'm not ready to be touched yet. Can you wait until I'm eighteen?"

He repeated what I said, and added, "Oh wow…I can't make that promise. Once we get married, you're going to be my wife and we have to do it."

I begged him in a low voice, blushing hard: "I'm just not ready."

He said, "That's not possible. I have to prove your virginity to my aunt. According to her, you're not even a virgin, but I know you are. So, I'm going to prove her wrong."

And that was that.

One day, Omar wanted to go to the park with me. I didn't feel comfortable going alone with him, so I took my little sister Adia with us. As we were sitting on the grass watching Adia play on the slides, he started to touch my hair. I wanted him to stop but he wouldn't. I asked him to stop, but by accident, I called him 'Zabi'.

I apologized, but Omar wasn't mad. He had known about Zabi's family's proposal. He told me he understood, and took the opportunity to make a confession. He told me that he was only marrying me because that's what his family wanted. He had a girlfriend back home, an American girl named Candy, and he was in love with her. He told me he was going to call her to tell her that he loved her and call off our wedding.

He did go to a pay phone after that, supposedly to call her. But afterwards, he acted normal and never said anything to anyone. I never found out what he said to her, if anything— but the planning for our wedding continued.

Looking back, I think I called him 'Zabi' because Zabi was still on my mind. If my parents had let me live my life the way I wanted, then I might have married Zabi after I was done with school and established a career the way I dreamed of. To this day, I wonder what might have happened if my life had taken that path instead of the one my parents chose for me.

October 1986 engagement party 5 days after Omar's arrival to Frankfurt, Germany

The sixth day of Omar's visit was the first time he hit me. He wanted to go visit one of his uncles, a man in his fifties whom I too called 'Uncle', since he was my stepmom's older brother, to invite him to our wedding. I told him I highly doubted that this uncle would come, since my stepmom was currently embroiled in some kind of argument with him; they weren't talking at the time. He said, "I know—that's why I want to go invite him in person."

When he came back, I asked what happened. He replied that his uncle had said to him, "I can't believe you're marrying my leftover."

I asked, "What does that mean—*leftover*?"

He said that his uncle told him that he'd had a lot of fun with me, touching and squeezing me. I still didn't understand, so I repeated what he told me and said again, "I don't understand."

I did remember that this uncle would always ask my sister Sophia and I to massage his back and neck; if we did, he would give us a dollar for ice cream. This in itself wasn't usual, but many years later, Sophia shared with me that he did sexually harass her. She was too scared to say anything about it to anyone. But at the time I didn't know about this and was genuinely baffled by my uncle's comment.

I told Omar, "If that's the case, that he would say something so disgusting, maybe he shouldn't be invited."

Omar replied, "I don't care what you say, he's still my uncle and I would like him to be there."

That made me very angry. I told him, "You're not a true man for saying this! The guy just insulted your future wife to your face."

Before I knew it, he slapped me—so fast and so hard that he bruised my face instantly. You could see the fingerprints.

Strangely, even in my shock I knew exactly what he was about to do next: hold me and speak sweetly to me to try and make up for it. This was a routine I'd seen my father doing it with both of his wives.

I cried and told him he'd hurt me; he apologized and said, "Try to cover the mark with make-up. I don't want anyone to see." Already a dutiful wife, I did as he said. I covered the bruising on my face and told no one what had happened.

After all was said and done, within ten days of Omar's arrival—on October 10, 1986—I got married in a kindergarten lunchroom in front of about sixty guests. My stepmom cooked the food with some help from her friends.

October 1986 leaving for the mosque for our Nikah

October 1986 leaving for the mosque for our Nikah

October 1986 our wedding day in the kindergarten hallway

October 1986 at our wedding

*October 1986 leaving our wedding to go to my parents'
friend's house for the night*

The wedding was hell, and I hated every moment of
it. I was wearing five-inch heels for the first time, and an ill-

fitting wedding dress; it was a size six, when I was an extra-extra small. My sister and I had to pin my dress right before I walked down the aisle. The dress was Omar's sister's that they'd brought for me; I had never tried on the dress, let alone seen it before. I did my own make-up, copying from a Dior brochure. Getting my hair done was a nightmare. My stepmom thought that paying thirty dollars to get it done was too much money.

Before the wedding, I cried to Omar that my hair was too thick and long for me to do by myself. He felt badly and gave me the money to get it done, but I ended up looking like the mom from the movie *Psycho*.

The worst part was after the wedding, when we were delivered to one of our parents' friends' houses to sleep. The couple had two small children; they slept in their kids' room, while we stayed in their bedroom.

I was still in the wedding dress as we walked into their small two-bedroom house. Omar quickly excused us from the living room to go to the bedroom. As we walked into the room, my heart was beating so fast and hard, and my palms were sweaty. I had never been this nervous or scared, and yet very embarrassed and shy. I didn't know what to do with this mix of emotions.

I didn't feel comfortable taking my clothes off in front of Omar. I was waiting for him to turn the lights off so I could get undressed, but he refused. He said, "Let me help you. Don't worry, I promise I won't bite. I'll just unzip your dress."

As soon as he started to touch me, I began shaking. The tremors seemed to come from deep down inside me. My body felt like I was on fire. I thought, *this would be a good time to die.* I didn't even care from that moment on whether or not I was alive.

I took the dress off and told him, "Please turn around." I didn't want him to see my body. But he didn't turn around—he watched me undress.

After I'd crawled into bed, he did what he'd said he was going to do. No matter how much I begged him not to touch me, it didn't matter to him. It was an awful and painful experience for me.

The next day, out of shame, I couldn't leave the bedroom. I didn't know how to face the couple I called my uncle and aunt, knowing that they were aware of what had happened in their bedroom last night.

The aunt ended up coming to the bedroom to get me. They offered us breakfast, but we had to leave to go back home. Omar told me on our way home that he was excited to show the proof of my virginity to my stepmom—yet another embarrassment for me.

Two days later, I flew with Omar and his father to Los Angeles, California. We got picked up from the LAX airport by his younger sister and younger brother. We drove to his older brother's apartment for dinner, then to his house later. He lived with his parents, his two younger brothers, and their spouses. Their house was large: about 3,000 square feet. It had two stories with four bedrooms, each room occupied by a couple. Our room was over the garage door. The garage had been turned into a party room, since they entertained often. The house seemed so big to me; my home in Germany had been a single-story half the size.

The next morning, when we woke up, Omar told me he was going to shower and go to work. I didn't want him to leave me there. I didn't feel comfortable, and it didn't feel like home to me. It felt more like I was visiting his family. As I went down, I heard everyone chatting, laughing and having breakfast. This made me feel a bit more at ease, but it also made me miss my family—especially Sophia, who I already had so much to tell. I also missed my baby brother Sal, who I'd raised like my own child.

When I came into the kitchen, everyone was kind and welcoming. My mother-in-law offered breakfast. My father-in-law asked if I'd slept well. I could barely keep up with them all. There were way too many people around. This was not like what I was used to at home, and I felt overwhelmed. Shortly after that, everyone started to leave for work.

Around the same time, my older brother-in-law and his wife dropped off their two small children, ages four and two, for my mother-in-law to babysit while they worked. A few minutes later, another sister-in-law and her husband dropped off their set of one-year-old twins and their two-year-old toddler. I was very confused. I couldn't imagine how my mother-in-law could take care of all five of these small kids. I was already missing my young half-siblings, so I offered to help. She told me, "Sure, but they've recently been fed and changed, so for now I could use your help with cleaning the upstairs while I clean downstairs."

I said, "Sure, what would you like me to do?"

She gave me a list: she wanted me to clean the two full bathrooms, including scraping the showers and tub. Then I was to Windex all of the closet mirrors in all four bedrooms and dust the furniture. Finally, she wanted me to vacuum the upstairs. She said, "By the time you get done with that, the kids will be ready for us to feed and their diapers will need changing."

These tasks were familiar to me, since I'd done so much cleaning when I lived with my stepmom. This would be the same, except that this house had more rooms. I was always a neat freak, so I took my time and made sure I cleaned to my own satisfaction—and, more importantly, my mother-in-law's. My first day as a bride went by cleaning and taking care of all the babies.

This became my regular schedule. It felt like a repeat of the life I'd had in Germany—but now I didn't have my sister, and I didn't get to go to school. I was in a strange country with no family or friends. I had no language, no money, no car, nowhere to go, and no one to talk to for an escape. I became very stressed and lonely.

On our second night of marriage, my husband started going out after work. He would call me almost every night to tell me that he'd be coming home late. I didn't like this, but I was too scared to say anything, and I knew that it would get me nowhere. It seemed like his parents believed anything their adult kids told them, so I kept my mouth shut.

But what I hated the most was sleeping with my husband. He would come home in the middle of the night drunk, smelling like pot and women's perfume, wanting to have sex with me. He did this every night, and if I ever pushed him away or pretended I was asleep, he would hit me and hold my mouth. I couldn't fight him, even if I tried. He would only hurt me more. Then he would rape me. Afterwards, if he heard me crying, he would grab me by my hair, drag me out of the room to the hallway and lock the door. He would say, "You want to cry? Now you can do whatever the fuck you want. I need to sleep. I have work tomorrow."

After a while, I learned to just let him do whatever he wanted to me. I would cover my face with a pillow to avoid seeing or smelling him. I chose to endure the rape without crying, rather than being hit and sleeping in the hallway.

After a month or so, while Omar was at work, his uncle Zamir came to see me. I really liked him; I had met him briefly in Germany before he moved to the US, and remembered him being very kind to my sister and I. He asked me if I was going to their cousin's wedding, to which we'd recently been invited. I said, "I don't know, because I don't have a dress to wear."

He said, "Why don't you get ready? I'm taking you shopping."

I was almost in tears—no one had ever taken me shopping like that before. I quickly got ready and he took me to Montclair mall, not too far from our home. When we got to the store—Broadway, a nice department store—I started to look through the dresses. Then I noticed a huge white teddy bear almost my size. I instantly fell in love with this bear. I stopped looking at dresses and told Omar's uncle that I'd changed my mind—I didn't want to go to the wedding anymore. I said I would rather stay home. Instead of the dress, I wanted the teddy bear.

He looked at me with a smirk and said, "What do you want to do?"

I repeated and said, "I would rather get this bear instead of a dress if that's ok? I really don't care to go to the wedding."

"Are you sure?" he asked.

I nodded. "Yes, I'm 100% sure."

He said, "Okay, if that's what you want, then I'll get you the bear." He ended up getting me a dress too; I guess he felt bad for me.

That day, I felt like the happiest girl in the world. I suddenly didn't feel alone anymore. I couldn't wait to get home. I was already thinking of the teddy bear as my new best friend; I had so much I wanted to tell him. Since I'd always loved horses, I named him Pony.

Pony become my obsession. We spend a lot of time together—especially the nights when Omar was out partying, which was almost every night. We slept together; we listened to sad songs and cried to them; he was the only one who knew all about me.

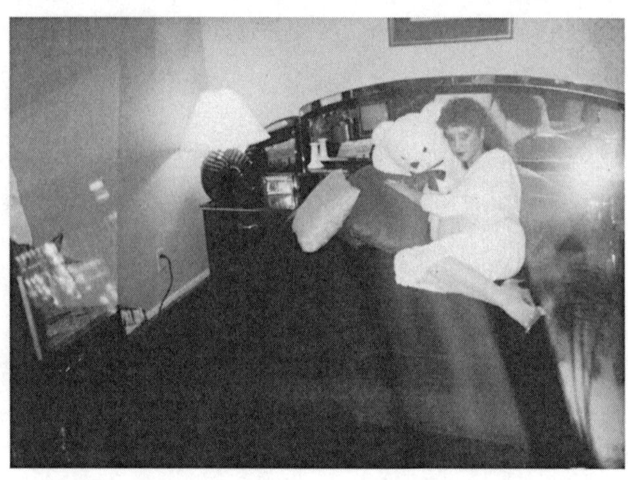

November 1986 in my bedroom with my Pony and wearing the dress Zamir bought me

One night Omar got mad at me because Pony was always in between us in bed, which made it harder for him to sleep with me. Out of nowhere, he lunged at Pony and ripped him in half. He did it so fast that it was too late by the time I tried to save him.

I was devastated. It seemed like within seconds my life had turned upside down. I cried and cried. The more I hugged and caressed Pony, the madder Omar got. He got out of bed, grabbed me by my hair, and threw me out of the room as I was holding Pony, trying to keep all of the stuffing from falling out of his body. I felt like Pony was dead; I felt so guilty seeing him hurt like that. I cried the entire night holding Pony and apologizing to him. It seemed like life without him was meaningless. Looking back, I was just a sixteen-year-old kid who needed a friend.

After that, I started to feel like I was done with life. I couldn't bear the situation my parents had put me in. I remembered how one of my friends had told me, *if you ever want to kill yourself, you can painlessly swallow a sewing needle*. So, I thought about it, and it didn't take too long for me to make my decision.

One night, while my husband was at work, his parents and I were home as usual. I borrowed his mom's sewing kit and went into my room. I took a needle out of the kit and stared at it for a while. Then I put it in my mouth and swallowed.

I waited a while before I went downstairs. I was starting to get scared of what would happen next. I told my father-in-law, "I accidentally swallowed a sewing needle."

He asked, "How?"

I told him, "I had the needle in my mouth as I reached on top of my closet shelf to get something, and it went straight down my throat really quickly."

He believed me. He sounded shocked and told me, "When Omar gets home, he has to take you to the emergency room, because this can kill you."

An hour or so later, when Omar got home, his dad told him, "You have to take her to the hospital."

I could tell Omar was pissed. He looked at me and said, "What happened?" and I just told him the same thing I'd told his dad.

We went to the hospital, and the doctor ordered an X-ray. He looked at it and said, "We can see the needle, but hopefully it should come out when she goes to the bathroom." He instructed me to go home and eat some bread and water—that would help to push it down. A part of me was disappointed, but also somehow relieved. I didn't want to go back to my miserable life, but there were some potential upsides to living: perhaps I would get to see my sister again.

The next day, I woke up and found myself alive, but confused. All I knew was that I didn't want to be in that house or around those people. I just wanted to disappear, but didn't know where.

As it happened, the needle never passed out of my body, and today, thirty-six years later, it's still inside of me. At one point, I looked into having it removed surgically, but I was told by the surgeon that that would be impossible, and at this point I just have to live with it. In the meantime, I can't get any MRIs done, because they could magnetize the needle and puncture an artery. That first botched suicide attempt is something I'll have to live with for the rest of my life.

Within three months of my arranged marriage, my father came to visit from Germany. My visa was expiring, so we needed to apply for my citizenship. Since I was underage in California and my marriage wasn't recognized as legal, the plan was to drive to Las Vegas and get married there. My father needed to be there to approve the marriage, since I was still a minor.

My father was in the States for a couple of weeks, but I almost didn't care to see him. I was very angry with him for putting me in my current situation. Yet I was still also very frightened of him; I'd grown used to him hitting me whenever my stepmom wasn't happy with me, or when I made a mistake or forgot to do something. To me he was just like my husband.

My dad and my father-in-law left for Las Vegas a day prior to us, so they could gamble; Omar and I left when he got off work. We were scheduled to get married the next day at Circus Circus. I had chosen that casino so I could play in the arcade afterwards.

Our drive was four hours long. I brought the first and only Barbie I'd ever owned. I'd bought her with my own pocket money, about three weeks before the trip. I'd named her Jassmine. She was beautiful, with dark skin and long black hair. I had a little hair brush for her, with a set of hair clips and a couple of different outfits. In the absence of flesh-and-blood friends, Jassmine was all I had, especially since I'd lost Pony; I pretended she was a real girl and told her all of my stories.

Omar always drank beer whenever he was driving. He always had a six-pack of Corona in his car. I absolutely hated it. I hated the smell of alcohol, and I hated the strange way people acted when they drank. I frequently told Omar that I didn't like him drinking, but it didn't matter what I said. He always just did what he wanted to do.

He had already gone through his fourth bottle when he asked me to get him another bottle from the back seat. I told him, "No, you've had enough."

He suddenly slapped me with the back of his hand on the side of my face. My lip started to bleed. I dropped Jassmine on my lap; he quickly grabbed her and threw her out the window. One minute she was on my lap, the next she was gone. In that moment, the last shred of my childhood was lost.

Everything happened so fast; so much was going on in my head in that split second. I tried to jump out of the window after Jassmine, but Omar grabbed my shirt and pulled me in. While half my body was still out the window, he closed and locked it. I couldn't roll the window down, so I opened the door to try and get free. All this time, he was driving seventy or eighty miles per hour. So much was happening. There was a lot of pulling, pushing and hitting.

Finally, Omar slowed the car down and stopped by the side of the road. I got out and ran toward where I thought Jassmine had fallen, crying hysterically. I just couldn't let her go like that. But Omar caught me, knocked the living daylights out of me and told me to get back into the car. He obviously was much stronger than me, and finally I obeyed.

The whole rest of the way to Las Vegas, I was bawling so hard, missing my Jassmine. I didn't want to get married in Circus Circus. I just wanted my bed and to be alone. But I was stuck in the car with him. My head and body felt like someone had hammered me from head to toe. Every part of my body was aching; my lips were lumpy and bleeding, and my face felt fat. When I looked at myself in the car mirror, I looked like a zombie, with bruises, a cut lip and a swollen face. I felt hopeless and worthless. Nothing made sense to me.

As we drew closer to our hotel, Omar suddenly started being nice to me. He was trying to force himself on me, touching my thighs and smiling, as if everything was just fine. I couldn't stand him. I wanted to hurt him so badly, but I knew there was nothing I could do. I tried to push him away, but he didn't care. He always did what pleased him.

We arrived at our hotel and he checked us into the room. He told me he was going to find our dads, but I just wanted to shower and be in bed. I cried myself to sleep.

I woke up the next day feeling like dead meat, but I had to get up. I covered my bruises with make-up and got ready quickly. At this point, I didn't care how I looked. I just wanted to put the wedding behind me and go back to California.

We got there right before noon. Omar's brother's sister in-law was there; she had brought me her wedding dress to wear so we could take pictures. This was the second time I'd had to wear another woman's borrowed wedding dress. This one was so big that it looked like a maternity wedding dress.

December 1986 at Circus Circus in Las Vegas,
legalizing our marriage

I remember thinking to myself, *at least the other dress didn't make me look like a pregnant little girl*. But at the same time, I honestly didn't care.

The funniest part about the whole wedding was that when we were in city hall to sign our marriage certificate, the worker pushed the certificate toward my dad, thinking my dad was my husband. I couldn't help but laugh. It made him mad, but I knew that in that moment he couldn't hurt me. Finally, we drove back home to California.

A day before my dad was scheduled to fly back to Germany, he told us that he would rather go and spend that night with his other sister-in-law in Inglewood. Her home was a lot closer to LAX. He asked me if I wanted to go stay there with him for the night. I asked Omar and he told me, "Sure, why not? I'll come after work and stay with you. We'll go back home the next day when your father leaves."

When Omar came over after work to the house in Inglewood, he had dinner with us. Shortly afterward, he told me he had to leave. He said he couldn't stay the night with me because he had work early the next day. This seemed strange to me, but I had to say okay—so he left.

An hour or so later, my father looked at me and said, "You know, I want to take you back home to your husband." He insisted, so I agreed. As we approached the house, Omar's car was parked in the driveway, but he wasn't home.

His parents were sleeping, but my sister-in-law Deepa was up. I asked her, "Where's Omar?"

She told me that he was at one of the video stores his family owned. "He came to the store, and told me I could drive his car home. He said he would have Mark drop him off later." At that moment it became obvious that Omar had lied to me. I instantly had a bad feeling; I knew he was up to no good.

I told my dad, "It's late, you should go to sleep." Then I went to my room, opened my curtains, and just sat there looking out the window, waiting for Omar to be dropped off. Around 3:45 a.m., an old blue Volkswagen pulled into the driveway. Omar was driving. After he got out of the car, he went around and opened the front passenger door—something I always asked him to do for me, which he always refused.

My heart dropped. I couldn't believe what I was witnessing. I saw a tall, beautiful blonde girl get out of the car. She looked around Omar's age, in her late twenties. I ran downstairs and hid myself behind the wall by the front door. At this point, Omar had no idea my dad and I were home. He opened the front door and walked in without seeing me. He went around the garage to bring the woman in through that door.

As soon as they came in, I came out from my hiding place and stood between them. They both looked like they'd just seen a ghost, especially Omar. He was at a loss for words.

The girl was so much taller than me. I had to crane my neck to look her in the eye. Just as I was about to tell her who I was, Omar introduced me by my name. I looked from him back to the girl. I said, "I am his wife!" and ran back inside the house, crying.

I was devastated. I couldn't believe he was cheating on me when that was the one thing I had told him not to do. The only thought going through my head was *I want to end my life*.

I decided to jump out of the bathroom window. I went straight to my room and grabbed my tennis shoes—I still don't know why I felt I had to put my shoes on—and went to the bathroom. I looked out the window. The fall seemed far enough to kill me, and the ground below was concrete.

Omar ran after me and knocked on the bathroom door. I was crying and putting my shoes on. I said, "I'm not opening the door! I'm going to jump out of the bathroom window to kill myself!"

It was one of those tiny bathroom windows; I knew I could fit through, since I was very small. But as I looked down, it seemed too high and scary. I just couldn't do it. I knew I wanted to die, but I still didn't want to feel any pain. I heard him leave. I figured he was going to go in the backyard under the bathroom window so he could maybe somehow save me. I left the bathroom and quickly ran to my bedroom. I thought, *maybe I can jump from my bedroom window, since it's not as high?*

I stood there, getting ready to jump. As much as I wanted to end my life, I was terrified. Looking down at the concrete, I just couldn't do it. I was picturing the pain I'd once felt when I broke my foot. I didn't want to go through that pain again in case I didn't die.

As I stood looking down, I heard the bedroom door open. I knew it was him. The last thing I wanted was for him to save me. So I quickly jumped.

I don't know how, but as I was in the air, I changed my position to the right. I ended up falling on the grass, and only hurting my feet a little. Shortly after, I was able to walk, though I had some pain in my ankles.

By the time all this happened, it was 6:00 a.m., and I couldn't stop crying. My dad was awake now and demanded to know what was going on. Through my tears, I shared with him some of Omar's abuse, from the first time he hit me a day before our wedding in Germany until a couple of days before my father had arrived. I told my father that I wanted to go home. Even though going home wasn't any better, I was very upset that Omar had cheated on me. My father tried to calm me down and offered to take me with him to one of his friends' house.

We went to the house of Uncle Sonna, who we knew from Germany. He and his wife had two sons around my age; we used to play together every time our parents were together and would stay weekends at each other's houses. When we got there, Uncle Sonna's wife was cooking in the kitchen. Her son Anil was home, so my dad left me with them and went with Uncle Sonna to reschedule his flight, since he'd missed it that morning. Anil asked me if I wanted to play cards with him. I could tell he was trying to keep my mind off things. Even though I didn't really care to do anything, I agreed to play.

As we were playing, we heard the door ring. Anil got up and opened the door. I heard Omar's voice, which gave me the chills. He shut the door and told me, "It's Omar. He wants to talk to you."

I told him, "Oh no. There's no way! I can't talk to him. He's going to hurt me now, especially since I'm here and he saw me playing cards with you. He's going to make me pay for leaving him." My stepmom had told Omar in Germany that I had some kind of a relationship with Anil, which of course I never did. He'd always been like a brother to me.

Omar heard me through the slightly cracked door. He shouted, "I promise I won't hurt you. Just come out! I just want to talk to you."

He kept on insisting until Anil finally said, "Go see what he's got to say, and I'll warn him not to touch you."

I looked at him with teary eyes and said, "Okay, but please make sure you stay close to the door. If anything happens, you need to come out and help me." He promised.

I went outside but left the door cracked open. Omar noticed; he immediately pulled me aside and shut the door. At first he just looked at me very angrily and chewed his lips, without saying anything. I thought, *Maybe I should speak?* But before I had a chance to open my mouth, he lifted his arm and slapped me so hard that everything around me suddenly turned black.

My head was spinning and my face felt heavy. My jaw felt loose and long. My lip started to bleed, but then it all went numb and hot. I wasn't sure what was happening with my face, but it felt pretty scary. It happened so fast I couldn't scream even if I had wanted to.

I touched my face and my hands came away covered in blood. I thought he must have broken my nose. I quickly managed to get away from him. I opened the door and got inside. I was holding my face with both hands, and there was blood dripping from between my fingers as I ran to the bathroom. I needed to see what he had done.

I quickly washed the blood off and looked in the mirror. I looked like the Elephant Man. My jaw had moved to the left side of my face, my lip was three times bigger than its normal size, and my nose was big and fat. The only thing I recognized was my eyes. All I could think was *how am I gonna face people*? I looked so scary. I couldn't cry, since it made the pain worse.

When Anil saw my face all bloody, he got scared and called the police. When they arrived, Anil told them what Omar had done to me. They immediately arrested him. When I saw him sitting in the back seat of the police car, handcuffed, I felt bad for him. I begged the officer, "Please release him! Just make him promise that he'll never hit me again."

She couldn't believe what I was asking her. She looked at me as if I was crazy and said, "The only thing you need to be concerned about right now is yourself. The ambulance is on its way. You need to go to the hospital."

I still begged and begged while I was holding my jaw; it hurt every time I tried to talk. She told Omar, "It's against the law for a husband to hit his wife. No matter what you say, there's nothing I can do."

The ambulance arrived and took me to the hospital. The doctor ordered an X-ray, which revealed that my jaw was broken. He told me, "There's nothing we can really do about a broken jaw. You're just going to need to go home and rest. You can't eat anything chewy or hard, so only liquids for the next eight weeks."

As I was waiting for my paperwork to get released, I saw Omar walking toward me. My heart dropped. It turned out his dad had bailed him out of jail.

I vaguely remember him having to take some anger management classes after that, but that was his only punishment. Now, looking back, it stuns and angers me to think that the medical staff would have allowed me to go home with him the day after what had happened.

But in the moment, I wasn't thinking about laws or hospital protocol; all I knew was that I was terrified. I didn't know how he was going to behave.

Surprisingly, he was calm. He apologized and said he'd do whatever I wanted him to do. He begged for me to come back, and promised that he'd never hit me again.

I felt like I had no good options at that point. Even if I went back home, things wouldn't be easy with my stepmom. I had missed so much of school, lost my virginity, and lost my sister; she had also been married off to an older man. So I decided to trust Omar, under one condition: that we could stay at his older brother's house until we got our own place. I knew if I went back to his parents', they might blame and punish me for their son's arrest. I felt somewhat more comfortable at Omar's brother's, since I was friends with his wife. She was much older than me, but I liked her; she was kind and sincere. He agreed and took me straight to his brother's house.

A couple of days later, my father returned to Germany. His parents started to talk about having a welcoming party for us, once my jaw healed, since they'd never held any formal celebration for us. If anyone thought it was odd to celebrate a marriage in which the husband had just been arrested for domestic violence, they didn't say so. At least in my presence, no one in his family ever acknowledged what had happened.

My reprieve from Omar's violence only lasted until my jaw healed. Within a couple of days, he took me back to his parents' house. He didn't discuss it with me beforehand—he just told me we were going there for dinner. After dinner I helped his mom in the kitchen, doing dishes. Once I finished, I told him I was ready to go back to his brother's house. He responded, "No, we're not going back there."

That made me very upset: I couldn't believe he had lied to me. I told him, "Fine. If you're not gonna take me, then I'll walk." And I did. I left his parents' house and started walking back to his brother's, which was about a fifteen-minute drive away.

After about twenty minutes of walking alone through the dark streets, I grew scared. Part of me wanted to get kidnapped and killed, just to make him feel guilty. With all these thoughts in mind, I heard a car slowing down next to me. I had never been this scared. I thought to myself, *Okay, Laila, you're getting what you asked for—now deal with it.*

With my heart in my stomach, I turned my head a little to look at the car. I saw a man in the driver's seat, but I couldn't make out his face. When he noticed me looking at him, he pulled closer to me. My heart pounded harder than ever as he rolled down his passenger window and yelled, "Get in the car!"

I was so scared I didn't recognize the voice. Then he started calling me by name, and I realized that it was Omar's younger brother Simon (no relation to my childhood sweetheart). I got into his car, went back to his parents' house and that was it—back to the reality I'd tried to leave behind.

The next day, Omar called from work. He said, "I'm going out and won't be home until later. You don't need to wait for me." I knew he was just going back to his old self. I was in bed tossing and turning, thinking, *if this guy comes home and tries to touch me drunk, I'll have to really end this life I'm in.* I didn't see my life getting better, only worse. I found myself hopeless again.

He finally got home around 3:00 a.m. and came to bed. He started to grab me and undress me, but I refused. I pushed him away, and that pissed him off so badly that he couldn't behave himself. He started to hit me in any way he could, then raped me. It was the same cycle as always. He threw me out of the room when he was done so he could sleep and my crying wouldn't keep him up.

The next day was the formal party for us that his family had been planning. During the day, as I was doing all the chores his mom asked me to do, I was brainstorming how to end my life. So far, I had tried the sewing needle and jumping from the second story, neither of which had worked. *What else could I do that would really kill me?* I came up with the idea of taking pills.

I remembered that my father had given me a bottle of heart pills for my father-in-law; when I read the instructions, it said, *Do not take more than one pill a day.* I counted twenty-five pills in the bottle. I figured this could be it. If I took the entire bottle, it should be enough to kill me. Around 4:00 p.m., I told everyone I was going to shower and get ready. That would give me a couple of hours before anyone would start asking for me. I had it all planned out. I took all of the twenty-five pills, took my shower, got dressed and lay in bed. Now it was an hour later, and I wasn't feeling anything yet.

Around 5:30 I started to feel a little strange. I went to Deeba, Simon's fiancée; she was getting ready in her room, right next to mine. The party was also for her and Simon, since they had just gotten engaged. I went to her room and made her swear to me that she'd keep what I told her a secret. After a few minutes of making her swear to me over and over, I finally told her what I had done. She was shocked; she couldn't believe it. I told her once I was dead, she could let everyone know why I'd done it. She promised me, and I felt good about telling her. I wanted Omar to know the reason.

Around 7:00 pm, I started feeling very sick. I felt like throwing up, but had no energy to move my body. My entire body felt limp, except my brain. I somehow managed to crawl halfway to the hallway to go to the bathroom; it must have taken me 20 minutes, though it was only 10 feet away. I was hearing all kinds of noises downstairs. I also heard Shan, Omar's eldest brother, come into the hallway.

When he noticed me on the floor, he asked me what was wrong. I could barely move and couldn't talk. My mouth just wouldn't move and my voice was very low and shaky. It was hard for me to even understand myself.

I whispered, "Please help me," but he couldn't understand what I was saying.

He asked me, "What's wrong?" but I could barely push any sound out of my mouth. I was trying to make eye contact with him, but I couldn't move; my body felt like lead. What I was experiencing was beyond my imagination. All I had wanted to do to die easily, but this was worse than Omar breaking my jaw.

The next thing I remember was hearing all kind of noises and seeing a blur of doctors and nurses around me. I went in and out of a daze. I hazily saw Deepa at my bedside. She was staring at me and crying.

The next day, I woke up feeling exhausted. I didn't know where I was. I felt weak and couldn't quite get my head up, but from what I could see, it looked like a hospital bed. I had wires stuck to my chest and my arms. For a second I was lost in my thoughts, but then I quickly remembered how I'd tried to commit suicide. I was disappointed: once again, I hadn't made it to death. Tears were falling down from the corners of my eyes. I felt scared. I knew that I was in more trouble than I could have ever imagined. I felt hopeless. I wasn't sure what was next for me.

As I was lost in my thoughts, I saw Omar walk through the door. He didn't say a word to me. The nurse told him he could take me home. She said that all I needed to do was to rest, and that I should be 100% okay in a couple of days. She had him sign some papers, and I was released. She wished me well as I left. Neither she nor anyone else at the hospital asked me why I had tried to kill myself; nobody inquired about my mental health or my situation at home.

Before I was able to put my seatbelt on in the car, Omar turned his body toward me, pulled his hand back as far as he could and slapped me. Then he started driving without saying a word.

When we got home his parents were sitting on the couch watching TV. I greeted them very softly, but they both ignored me. I felt like shit. Again, I just wanted to die. But it seemed like God wasn't going to let me go through with it. I went to my room and slept.

The next day, his parents again ignored my greetings and didn't talk to me at all. I already knew what was expected of me, so I did exactly that. I did my cleaning routine and took care of their five grandkids. I went through that for about a week, during which his parents continued to ignore me as punishment for trying to take my life. One of my sisters-in-law told me that if I wanted her parents to talk to me, I'd have to apologize. That wasn't easy for me, because I didn't attempt suicide out of pleasure. I wanted to kill myself because their son was physically and emotionally abusive. But I knew I couldn't argue, so I just apologized and kissed the back of their hands. I was forgiven.

A couple of weeks later, my sister Sophia called from Germany. She told me that she and her husband wanted to come and visit us. I couldn't believe it! I was so excited. I went around the house and told everyone that my sister was coming.

When I told Omar, he asked, "Where are we going to have them sleep?" That was the last thing on my mind, but he was concerned about it. He wanted them to have their own room, so he told me we needed to move before they arrived. I couldn't believe what I was hearing. This whole time, when I wanted us to get our own place, he would always say no. Now he wanted to? I told him that, of course, I was happy to move, but that we'd need some things for our new place. He said, "I'll figure something out."

October 1991 my sister Sophia with her husband and Diana in Hanover, Germany.

I was thrilled with this news. Not only would I get to see my sister, but I would also have my own place. We got a two-bedroom apartment not too far from his parents. His mom took me to the Pic 'N' Save store. We bought all the kitchen and some bathroom necessities. She gave us her old couch from her garage, and a couple of thin twin mattresses for my sister and her husband. We moved within days.

My sister and her husband arrived a couple of days after our move. It was her husband's first time in the US, so we wanted to go sightseeing. Omar decided to take us to the Walk of Fame in Hollywood when he was off work. After hours of walking and sightseeing, we were all very hungry. Omar refused to get us food. He said, "Let's go home and I'll make you guys some hamburgers."

When we got home, he asked for my piggy bank, where he would sometimes deposit stray coins. He said he needed money for the meat and buns. I was in disbelief—was he really that broke? There really wasn't much in the piggy bank—it amounted to maybe ten dollars. But he went to the store and got us some ground beef and buns.

I was kind of embarrassed, because my sister's husband kept bragging about money. I realized then that there was some competition going on between the brothers-in-law, but it didn't bother me. This was what it had taken for us to get our own apartment. All I really cared about was finding a way to be happy and not live in fear of him.

The day my sister left, we were both devastated. Our crying started days before, but the worst of it was her last day. I sobbed on our way to and from the airport, and I couldn't stop my tears for weeks.

Soon, I started feeling sick and throwing up for days on end. Omar took me to the doctor to see what was going on. After some blood work, they announced that I was pregnant. Omar showed a lot of excitement, but I was speechless. I wasn't sure how to process the idea of having a child and being a mother. It was very difficult, knowing the situation I was in.

When we moved, Omar and his dad had decided that I needed to work in one of their family video stores. The store was about forty miles each way from my apartment. I wasn't driving at that time, so my father-in-law would pick me up every morning at 9:00 a.m. to drive me to work. We would open the store a little before 10:00 a.m. and close at 10:00 p.m. Omar would pick me up after his workday ended.

Omar was a car salesman at a Toyota dealership, and he often worked late. He sometimes wouldn't pick me up until way after the video store had closed. I was always so scared to be alone in the store. Every time someone dropped their movies in the drop box, or I heard some drunks hanging around the shopping center, I would hide behind the counters on the floor and pray for Omar to come soon. Sometimes the drive back home with him was hell, too. He almost always drove drunk, with an open beer bottle next to him. Many times, I tried to jump out of the car while he was driving on the 210 freeway. I figured, *he's going to kill me driving drunk anyways. Why not just jump and do it myself?* If I was going to die, I wanted to kill myself rather than letting him kill me.

During my morning drive, I asked my father-in-law on at least three different occasions to pull over because I had severe morning sickness. One day he told me to bring plastic bags because he was tired of pulling over and delaying our arrival at the store. Pulling over was already embarrassing enough to begin with, but it was at least outside the car. Now I actually had to vomit right in front of him into a bag. It was a terrible feeling. I thought, *Why do they even want me to work when I'm this sick?* It wasn't like they were paying me. None of it made any sense. I felt stuck; I was just a sixteen-year-old pregnant girl who had nowhere to turn.

After three months of nonstop morning sickness, my father-in-law finally had the heart to tell me that I should just stay home and not work anymore. He said, "Since you're going to be home, I need you to cook for your husband." I agreed. I didn't mind cooking, though I knew I had a lot to learn.

On my first week of staying home, I got up every morning with Omar. While he showered, I would iron his work clothes: a collared shirt and slacks. Then I would make him breakfast.

One day, I wanted to surprise him with a nice dinner. I decided to make him Korma challow, a dish made with beef, tomato sauce and white rice. I knew he liked it when his mom made it, so I got the recipe from her. The problem was that we had no Basmati rice.

Since I didn't have a car, I walked to an Indian market about three miles away. It was a very hot summer day, and walking back I was carrying a ten-pound bag of rice, but somehow I made it. I started cooking and finished around 10:00 p.m. I was expecting him home around 10:30, but he didn't show up. By 11:00, I started to get worried. I called his uncle who worked at the same dealership, but he told me Omar had left before him. Next, I called his older brother Shan. I thought maybe Omar had stopped by to see him for a beer or something, but he also said he hadn't heard from him. I finally called back his work and the security guard answered. He responded, "I'm sorry, Miss. No one is here. The dealership is closed and all the employees have left." By then, it was midnight.

I was scared that something might have happened to him, but I also had a gut feeling that he was with his ex-girlfriend, Candy—the one he'd told me about before we got married. She wasn't the blonde woman I'd caught him with at our house that night, but I felt certain that he was still seeing her.

I waited. Now it was 1:30 a.m., and there was still no sign of him. The more I thought of him being with Candy, the more certain I became. My dinner was getting dry, and the table I'd fixed with burning candles started to look sad. I turned everything off, locked the door and left the apartment. I wanted to punish him. I thought *I'll just go somewhere and not be home when he shows up. He'll be worried, and maybe he'll never go out this late again.*

I went across the street, where there was a Rite Aid and some other small businesses. There was a bench I thought I could sit on and wait. As I approached the shopping center, I saw some people talking and hanging out in the parking lot. I thought *this might be good. I won't be alone.* But as I continued toward the bench, I realized that it was a group of drunk guys holding something in brown bags—alcohol, I assumed. My heart was beating so hard and fast that I could hear it. I wanted to run back, but I got scared; I thought if I ran, they might get curious and come after me. So I stayed calm and sat on the bench a few feet away from them. Before I knew it, they were trying to talk to me and ask me all kinds of questions. Some I understood, but some I didn't. My English was very rudimentary and I could barely answer them.

A million things were going through my head at that late hour. As much as I tried to look away and avoid eye contact with them, the guys were getting drunker and more obnoxious. I felt like my body was melting into the bench. I couldn't find the courage to move, but I was also afraid of what they'd do to me if I stayed any longer.

Somehow, eventually, I talked myself into finding the courage to get up and start walking back home. They called after me, "Hey pretty girl, where are you going? Why don't you stay and have a drink with us?" I just stayed silent and walked toward my apartment, looking back every so often to see if they were following me.

I made it home at 3:00 in the morning. I found my apartment still empty, with no sign of Omar. I was torn apart—mad at him and mad at myself. I couldn't believe that I had jeopardized my baby's life to teach him a lesson. But it felt so unfair: he just didn't have to experience the same worry he put me through. I lay in bed with my hands on my tummy, staring at the ceiling, waiting for him. Minutes felt like hours until I finally heard the door open. I looked at the clock; it was 4:30 a.m. I took a deep breath and turned sideways, facing the wall. I suddenly felt exhausted. I just wanted to close my eyes and go to sleep. I heard him walk into the bedroom, turn the bathroom lights on and start to get ready for bed. I pretended to be asleep, but of course, the second he got to bed, I smelled the strong stench of alcohol on him.

The bars and clubs closed at two, which meant he should have been home no later than three. I couldn't stand the idea of him being with someone else while I was pregnant with his child—especially after I'd spent the entire day cooking for him and making everything perfect.

I turned around and asked him, "Where were you?"

He responded, "I had to drive far to deliver a car for a customer."

I had to admit that this was a good lie. He thought I had no choice but to believe him. I just turned back around and didn't say anything. I was trying to figure out how I could catch him in the lie.

Suddenly overwhelmed with emotional exhaustion, I started to cry. Instead of comforting me or trying to explain himself, he exploded in anger, pulled my hair and dragged me out to the balcony, muttering that he couldn't sleep while I carried on like that.

He went back inside and locked the door behind him. I banged on the door for a while, but he ignored me. Eventually, I cried myself to sleep. I spent the next few hours out on the balcony by myself.

At eight in the morning, I heard Omar unlocking the patio door for me. I came inside without saying a word to him and I went to lay in bed while he took a shower. As I lay there, wide awake, I felt as if my whole world was a mess. I was desperate for answers, and my thoughts were running in 10,000 directions. I wanted so badly to escape, but now that I was pregnant, I felt more stuck in this life than ever.

I got up and made him some eggs with toasted bread and orange juice. I'd been told I had a duty to my husband to make him food after ironing his clothes each morning. I had it ready on the table, but he refused to eat it.

I noticed he was walking toward the front door, about to leave, so I told him, "Eat your food."

He said, "I don't want it," and left the apartment, starting to walk downstairs.

I quickly grabbed the plate of eggs, opened the door and said "Here!" Right when he turned, I threw the plate of food at him, and it got all over his shirt.

He looked up and said, "You fucking bitch! I'm gonna get you," and started running up the stairs. I quickly ran inside and locked the door, pulling the chain shut so that even if he used his keys, he couldn't get in. After a few minutes of cussing and kicking the door, he finally said, "I'll be back, bitch," and left.

Within an hour or so, I heard the doorbell. I tried to ignore it. I had a feeling it was him. A part of me wanted to open it, but I was too scared. I didn't know what he'd do. I got closer to the door and asked, "Who is it?"

I heard my father-in-law's voice. He said in a demanding tone, "Laila, open the door." I was already scared of him, and my culture told me I should always respect elders and in-laws no matter what. I gently opened the door without any hesitation. As he walked in, I saw Omar right behind him. I wasn't sure what was about to be said or done to me. Ignoring Omar, I greeted my father-in-law with a very calm and frightened voice: "Please have a seat. Would you like some tea?"

He replied, "No. I'm here to talk to you about what you did this morning. That kind of behavior is unacceptable. You must obey your husband. If you have a hard time doing that, I can easily send you back to Germany because there are a lot of girls like you out there. I can get one for fifty dollars."

I raised my head, trying not to cry, and looked at Omar for a brief moment; he just shook his head, confirming his father's words. After he was done lecturing and insulting me, they left.

My heart felt so heavy. I leaned against the front door, and my tears began to pour. My legs got weak and started to slide down to the floor. I cried so hard that I somehow fell asleep.

I woke up hours later, incredibly thirsty. I helped myself to a glass of water and took a few minutes to think about what had just happened. I tried to convince myself to accept what they wanted from me, but I knew it was impossible. I knew what I'd done that morning wasn't really my fault. I was so upset that Omar's dad didn't even want to know why I'd done it.

I felt so sad and lonely. I called my sister-in-law, Sima. She was married to the oldest brother and was the oldest sister-in-law. She was about twelve years older than me, and it seemed like Omar's family had a lot of respect for her. We got along well, and I could tell she'd been feeling badly for me. I sort of trusted her. I called her and shared everything that had happened the previous night and that morning. I cried my heart out to her and made her promise not to mention anything to her husband or the rest of the family.

She promised, so I asked her for a favor. I told her, "I've decided to terminate my pregnancy based on my marital problems…can you help me?"

Sima agreed to help and set up an appointment for me with her gynecologist. A couple hours later, she picked me up, drove me to the appointment, and helped me fill out some paperwork before I got called into the exam room. When I saw the doctor, he told me, "You're two weeks past the window for legal abortion. You are at fourteen weeks, and we can only do it up to twelve weeks. Anytime past that is against California law."

My first thought was *Oh my god! What do I do now? It can't get any worse. How am I going to survive this unwanted life with a baby?* Some part of me did feel relieved—the part of me that had already grown attached to the baby. But I didn't want to be a wife to Omar or a mother to his child, and now I had no option but to do so. I felt hopeless.

That night, when Omar came home from work, I started to question him about his night out the previous night. He obviously didn't know about the abortion idea. He swore to me up and down that he'd been delivering a car to a customer somewhere far away. He said, "I even have the paperwork in the car if you want. I can show it to you in the morning." I knew he was just stalling for time.

I couldn't sleep all night. The next morning, I asked to see the paperwork, because I knew he was lying. As I followed him to the car, I could tell he was very nervous. He got in the car and as he was about to close the door, I asked him to show me the paperwork. He was trying to ignore the reason why I was following him.

He showed me some paperwork, but it was dated a few days earlier. It didn't make any sense to me. When I brought the incongruent dates to his attention, he pushed me away with the car door so he could shut it and quickly take off.

I held on to the door, demanding, "Where were you really?"

He replied, "You stupid bitch. You don't know shit." He pushed me again, but this time harder, to hurt me. As he took off, he called me a 'fucking cunt'. At the time, I had no idea what 'cunt' meant, but it sounded bad.

Right when I got back to the apartment, I got a call from Omar's dad. He said, "Get ready. You're covering someone's shift." I was not in a good mental state to work, but of course, I couldn't say no.

Within thirty minutes of my arrival in the shop, the phone rang. When I answered, the woman on the phone asked, "Is this Laila?"

I said, "Yes, this is she. What can I do for you? May I ask whom I am speaking to?"

She replied, "This is Candy."

My heart instantly dropped and my whole body started to shake. I knew exactly who she was—Omar's ex-girlfriend, who he'd told me he no longer saw. She told me that she had been with him two nights ago. She said, "He offered to treat me for my birthday and take me to Disneyland. We spent a few hours in the Disney hotel afterwards… He told me that you two were no longer together and that he'd sent you back to Germany."

I couldn't believe what she was telling me. I told her everything. I told her how he was lying. I even told her that I was three months pregnant with his child. I could tell she was very sad and disappointed. I was dying to meet her just to see how she looked and behaved. I guess I was curious why he was still in love with her. I asked her if we could meet. She said "Okay, let me think about it, and I'll let you know." A couple of hours later, she called back and said, "I don't think it's a good idea to meet with you." I understood, but I was extremely upset about the whole situation. My husband was not only lying but was still seeing another woman. They'd been together in a hotel room while I was waiting for him with the food ready on the table and those drunk men out on the bench. I was dying to see him that night so I could tell him I knew everything.

When he came to pick me up, he had a six-pack of Corona in the back seat and was already on his second bottle, as usual. It stunned me how he could just take the chance of drinking and driving with his pregnant wife in the car. I must have stared at him long enough for him to know something was up. He kept on asking me, "What's that look about?"

I turned to him and said, "I know… I know everything." He acted like he had no idea what I was talking about. I finally told him, "Candy called me today and she told me everything you did for her birthday."

The look on his face was priceless. He was at a loss for words. I told him, "You have to choose: me and our baby, or her. If you choose me, I expect you to call her tomorrow and tell her that you love me and want to be with your family, and that you will never ever contact her again. If you choose her, then I'll terminate the pregnancy and go back home to Germany."

He stayed quiet and didn't say a word. Tears were falling down my face like heavy rain. I continued, "This morning, when you pushed me with the car door, you hurt my stomach. And your dad called me the other day and told me that there are a lot of girls like me out there for fifty bucks a month. Do you know how painful that was to hear? Why am I being compared to a prostitute? I'm only sixteen years old and was a high school student when you married me. Yet you were the one who didn't come home and went out with your ex-girlfriend. Then you lock me out on the balcony, leave me in the dark cold night with a little T-shirt on while I'm pregnant!" I realized that I was suddenly fearless; I was speaking up because I just couldn't take it anymore.

He didn't say anything in response, but he tried to put his hand on my lap and hold my hand. That was something he always loved doing when driving, no matter how much I pushed him away.

I just turned away. After telling him how I felt, I had no more tears to shed. We were both silent the rest of the way home.

I didn't say a word to him when we got home. I cleaned up and went straight to bed. I was exhausted. I felt so overwhelmed that I was praying for God to let me sleep forever. I didn't want to go on.

The next morning, I asked him, "Have you reached a decision? I want to know today. If you choose her, I need to make an appointment to terminate my pregnancy. If not, then I expect you to call her and let her know."

He replied, "Okay, I'll call her." I wasn't sure if he was actually going to tell her what I told him to say. He picked up our bedroom phone while I was listening on our living room phone.

It rang a few times before she answered, "Hello?"

When I heard her voice, my heart started to pound and my body started to shake and sweat. He told her almost exactly what I'd told him to say to her. All I heard her saying was "Okay." After the phone call ended, he came to me, hugged me and asked if I was happy.

I said to him, "It's too early. It'll take time for you to prove to me that you can be trusted."

After that, I began to see little changes in him. He started showing more interest in me and the baby inside me. But his contempt and mockery did not stop. Since I had never received much love, attention and care from anyone in my life, I was content with what I was getting. Was it enough? No, of course not. But it was better than what I'd had before. So I tried to accept this life, compared to what I could have had back in Germany.

Between the fifth and ninth month of pregnancy, things were up and down. Some days we were happy, but then some days he made me feel like shit. When I started showing, he constantly made fun of my weight. Although I had only gained twenty-five pounds of pregnancy weight, he started calling me 'Penguin'. When we fought, his refrain was "You worthless piece of shit. Look at yourself in the mirror, you cunt!" It would be another five years before I understood the meaning of that word, but I heard it all the time.

Every now and then, I would talk back, and then he'd beat me. He didn't go so far as to break my jaw or give me a concussion, but he would give me a hard slap on the face or pull my hair.

His mom once invited me over for lunch. She wanted to make me a special dish called Bolonie that most pregnant women crave. Without discussing it with me, he planned to drop me off at his mom's house for lunch and let me stay there until he got off work. Since I had the worst morning sickness in the first half of the day, I just wanted to be in bed and rest for the second part of my day. I didn't feel like staying the entire day at his mom's house. I also knew his mom would expect me to help clean her house and take care of her five grandkids.

I told him, "I would rather have you drop me back home after lunch."

He said, "I won't have any time to drop you back."

This made me very upset. I couldn't understand why he hadn't just asked me about it in advance. On the way there, we kept arguing. He was yelling and cussing and saying hurtful things, and I suddenly couldn't take it anymore. Without thinking twice, I opened the car door and tried to jump out while the car was in motion. He quickly pressed the brakes and I got out, shut the door and told him, "If that's the case, I'm going to walk to your mom's and walk back home."

He shouted, "Get back in the car! There's no way you can walk."

I refused. I told him, "I'll show you how," and just like that, he took off. I didn't think he would actually let a 6-month pregnant woman walk for over 2 hours in 90-degree heat, but he did.

Of course, my act of defiance didn't change the outcome. By the time I made it to his mom's house, I was hot and exhausted. Even if I could have mustered the courage to walk out of their house after lunch, I didn't have the energy. These small 'rebellions' of mine were the only way I could express opposition, but they almost never had any effect.

The day I went into labor was one of the most painful days of my life. My labor lasted over eighteen hours. I wasn't dilating after hours of walking and crawling on the hospital floors. Omar tried to be patient at first, but as the day wore on, he grew increasingly irritable. In the late evening, he tried to sleep, but my screams and moans kept waking him. More than once, he slapped me across the face to shut me up. Of course, he never did this when nurses or doctors were in the room.

Finally, when the doctor came in to check on me, I screamed: "Please do whatever it takes to get the baby out!" I thought I couldn't take any more of the pain.

He said, "You are way too young for a C-section. I'll give you another hour, and if you don't dilate by then, then I'll do the C-section." About thirty minutes later, my water broke. Thirty minutes after that, I finally delivered my little angel, Diana!

She was a perfectly healthy baby girl, twenty-one inches long and weighing seven pounds, fourteen ounces. When I saw her, my whole world suddenly changed; I forgot all about my problems in life, because all that mattered was her. I couldn't be any happier, and I couldn't wait to go home with her.

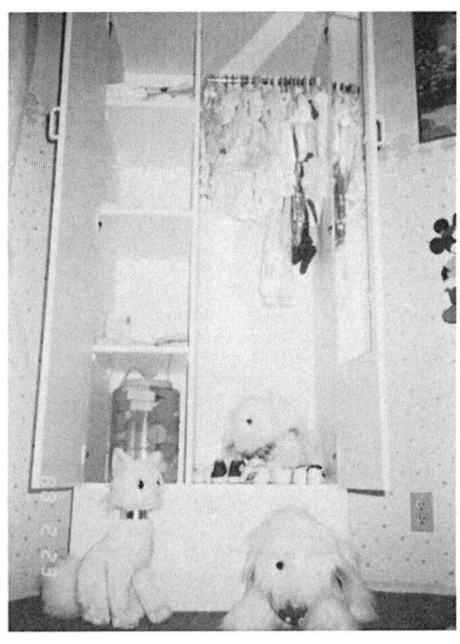

January 1988 my baby girl Diana's wardrobe

Two days later, we were released and went home. I already had Diana's nursery done; it looked just as beautiful as my baby girl, with matching bedding and wallpaper. She had a little closet with tiny pink-and-white baby hangers sporting many cute outfits and shoes, and a room full of toys. She had everything a little baby girl could possibly want.

The first six weeks after giving birth, I stayed with my dad and stepmom, who had recently moved from Germany, so I wouldn't be alone at home. My stepmom offered to help me with my baby (most days, Omar worked 14-hour shifts).

February 1988 with my baby girl Diana

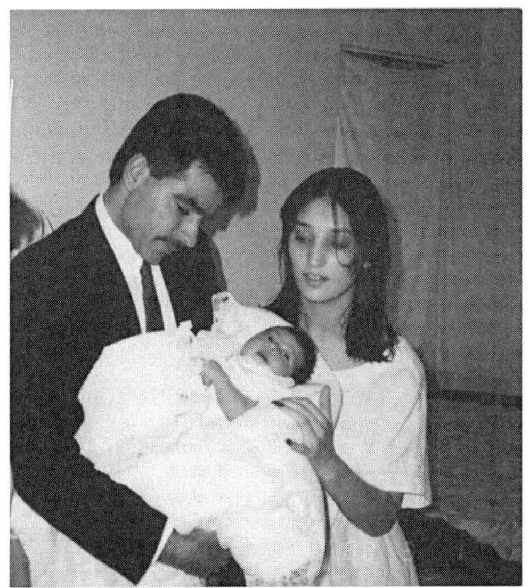

March 1988 with Omar and baby girl Diana

My second week after giving birth, Omar started pushing me to have sex when he got home from work, no matter how much I begged him to leave me alone. My stitches were still fresh and painful, and I could barely move myself or use the bathroom comfortably. But it didn't matter to him. He just wanted what he wanted.

At my six-week doctor's visit, the doctor checked me and Diana, and told me I was pregnant again. I was shocked and couldn't believe it. My first thought was that there was no way I could be a mother to two new babies back to back. Although Omar and my family begged me to keep it, I told my doctor I wanted to abort the pregnancy.

Finding myself in this situation made me think back to my own childhood. I questioned why my parents had wanted to have me. I hardly remembered them loving me or caring for me. They never did things like buying me toys or taking me to the park. It felt more like I was born to be their slave. This was perhaps one of the reasons why I felt worthless and often tried to take my own life. These thoughts made me feel certain that I didn't want to raise my kids the way I'd been raised; I wanted to give them everything that I'd never had.

But I knew I couldn't do so under these circumstances. I wasn't ready for another child yet. I had no other choice but to abort. The experience was very difficult, and I still live with the guilt, but I have forgiven myself for making the only choice available to me at the time.

June 1988 Diana in her crib

As the next few years went by, I was fully immersed in new motherhood. Meanwhile, Omar got a job working at

Longo Toyota, one of the largest dealerships in the world. He began to make good money, and by the time Diana was three years old, he was able to afford the down payment on our first home.

I loved furnishing and decorating our home. One thing that Omar loved and appreciated about me was my taste in decor; he would let me do whatever I wanted, and proudly showed off our home to his friends and family. He wanted to achieve all the American dreams: buying a house, then a new car for me.

Although it was nice to have my own home and car, none of that made much of a difference to me, because his behavior continued to be abusive, and I was deeply troubled by his increasing reliance on alcohol and drugs.

I remember the first time I filed for divorce. Diana was about three years old at the time. I had found a big Ziploc bag of weed in Omar's truck. When I confronted him about it, he denied that it was his. I told him how much I hate people doing drugs and that I wouldn't tolerate it. He just continued to deny it. I knew he was lying.

When he left for work, I searched the yellow pages and found a local lawyer. I called his office and they told me he was available and I could come to see him right then. I told the lawyer I wanted a divorce and explained why. He helped me begin the proceedings.

At the same time, I knew that if I was serious about leaving the marriage, I'd need to somehow get a job.

I had a stack of business cards from modeling and acting scouts; I was frequently approached and asked to audition, but Omar was always against it. He would tell me, "It's not because of your looks. It's only because they want to have sex with you." Even if it was an old overweight woman, he would still say that.

I called the numbers on a couple of those business cards. One of the agents I reached told me that they were looking for actors to audition for a milk commercial. The person over the phone gave me an appointment.

When I went, they put me in front of a camera with a milk commercial script. After a couple of tries, they told me that if the director liked me, I'd get a callback. To my surprise and delight, I did! I did well at the callback audition too. Soon afterwards, I heard the phone ring; when I picked it up, the first word I heard was "Congratulations!" I had booked the commercial.

Unfortunately, Omar was listening on the upstairs phone. He waited until the woman was done talking. Then he cussed her out, hung up and beat the crap out of me. I told him why I'd auditioned for the commercial: because I had filed for divorce and needed to be economically independent. After that, he slashed my tires, took my credit cards and cash allowance, grabbed his keys and left for work.

Needless to say, this was exactly the reaction I'd feared. My independence, economic and otherwise, was a threat to him; he'd do whatever it took to dissuade me from trying again.

That night, when he came home, I was in the kitchen washing dishes, about twenty-five feet away from him, while he was on the couch watching TV. I'd been ignoring him since he got home, and that made him mad. He grabbed a crystal ashtray that must have weighed five pounds and threw it at me. It hit my head so hard that I just dropped like a pile of dough onto the kitchen floor.

A few minutes later, I heard the sound of people and noises. I wasn't sure where I was. As I tried to open my eyes, I felt a heaviness and pain on the right side of my head. When I touched it, it felt bumpy. I was confused, but pretty quickly I remembered what had happened. I realized I was alone in the kitchen; Omar was still sitting on the couch, watching TV. I was amazed that he hadn't even cared to at least check on me when there was a chance that he could have killed me.

I somehow managed to get myself up and finish the rest of the cleaning. Tears were sliding down my face, but I kept quiet. I didn't want him to know I was crying; I tried to conserve my pride in any way possible.

When I woke up the next day, I had the worst headache I'd ever experienced. Omar never apologized; he just told me, "If you ever try this modeling shit one more time, I will tell everyone that you are leaving me so you can have the freedom to sleep with all the scouts to get modeling jobs."

I knew that by "tell everyone," he really meant telling my father. Knowing how abusive and scary my father could be and how prideful he was of his name, the last thing I needed was to get beaten by him too. I vowed to stay away from trying again, or even talking about acting or modeling. I felt defeated; the idea of escaping my marriage seemed farther away than ever.

Later that day, Omar called from work. Without acknowledging what he'd done to me the night before, he told me, "I'll meet you at your parents' tonight. They invited us for dinner."

With my headache, I was in no mood to be doing anything, but I knew I had no choice. As I stepped into my parents' house with Diana, the second my father laid eyes on me, I suddenly froze. I saw hate and anger flash across his face. He started to call me really bad names; he accused me of wanting to sell my body just to be on television, of trying to destroy his name.

He then quickly got up and ran toward the kitchen to grab a kitchen knife—whether to kill me or scare me, I don't know. His brother-in-law, who was there watching the scene, tried to stop him, while I ran out of the house as fast as I could, until I could no longer breathe, hear or see anything. My heart and head were pounding painfully.

After some time, while I was roaming the dark empty streets not knowing what to do, I saw one of Omar's uncles, whom I liked a lot, looking for me. He asked me to come back, that my father would not hurt me. But I was too scared to follow him inside. I told him I just wanted to take my daughter and go home.

I spent the entire night awake, in pain. The headache was only getting worse. My head felt like it weighed fifty pounds, and my body was exhausted. I knew had to go see my doctor.

The second she walked into the exam room, she knew. I had seen her for a couple of years now. In the past, I would mostly see her with Omar, since my English was broken. He would translate for me. This time, I was by myself. She asked, "What's wrong?"

I told her, "I've been experiencing extreme headaches on the right side of my head for the last couple of days."

She asked, "What happened?"

I said, "I just fell while skiing."

She didn't buy my story. She told me, "You can trust me. Tell me the truth so I can help you… Did your husband do this to you?"

I replied "No" and started to cry. I couldn't hold back my tears, but I refused to budge from my lie. Though I trusted my doctor, I was afraid that Omar would retaliate if he found out that I told anyone what had been going on in our marriage. When he'd been arrested for breaking my jaw, nothing had changed afterwards; he'd only had to attend anger management classes, which he resented doing and punished me for. It only made things worse. I had no faith that confessing my troubles to the doctor would result in a better outcome for me.

I was hospitalized for five days, then signed a consent form to be released. I didn't care to stay longer. All I cared about was going home and being with my baby girl.

After I came home, Omar continuously begged me to drop the divorce. At first I refused, so he escalated his tactics. He invited his grandmother to come down from San Francisco and try to talk me out of it. I'd always had a lot of love and respect for his grandma, so I agreed to talk to her.

I told her my reasons for filing for the divorce, narrating all of the abuse I'd suffered up to that point. She listened sympathetically, then asked me to reconsider. She promised that she personally would make sure that Omar's behavior changed, and that he would be a wonderful husband from that point on.

I felt I had no choice but to try and trust her. In our culture, it's so important to obey one's elders and do what they ask of you; standing up for myself against Omar was one thing, but opposing his grandmother would be another thing entirely. And of course I wanted to believe it was possible for him to change. I decided to give him another chance, and dropped the divorce. Now, looking back, I see how he manipulated the rules of our culture to get me to stay.

I decided to sign up for an interior design class at the local community college, Chaffey College. I'd always loved interior decorating from a very young age, and I was very good at it. People were always telling me I should be doing this for living, when they saw how I'd designed Diana's nursery and set up our new home. Design came very naturally to me; it was something that gave me a sense of freedom, control and independence. Above everything, I really enjoyed it.

After I signed up to start school, I told Omar about it. He didn't say anything to me, so at first I thought he was okay with it. Then, two days later, he came home carrying a huge bag. I asked him what it was. He said, "It's yours, why don't you open it?"

When I did, I found that the bag was filled with all kinds of beauty supplies, such as a dummy head, perm rods and rollers. He told me, "You're signed up to start beauty school next week."

I said, "But I want to do interior design!"

He said, "That'll never happen—there's no way you can do that. I want you to go finish beauty school, and once you're done, I'll open a salon for you. You're very good at doing hair and make-up—this will be perfect for you." It was true that I used to do make-up and hair for his sister, and sometimes some family friends, just for fun. He continued, "We have an appointment tomorrow for you to meet your principal and teachers." It seemed like that was that.

I started beauty school the following week. We found a babysitter for Diana from an ad. She didn't live too far from us, and I felt comfortable leaving Jaz with her since she was a stay-at-home mom of two young kids around the same age.

It was a ten-month program. Once I had completed my hours, I was very nervous to take the state board exam, since my English was still limited—but I studied hard and ended up passing it. It was very exciting for me.

Shortly after that, Omar opened up a hair salon in South Pasadena. He said it would be all mine and I could do whatever I wanted with it. But he also hired a manager named Dori and told me she was my boss.

I hadn't been particularly interested in owning my own business at the age of nineteen—I knew I wasn't ready for that kind of responsibility. Still, I resented that Omar had made me a false promise. After all, the seemingly generous gift of my own business ended up just being another way for him to control me.

On top of that, he hadn't really thought it through from a business angle. Sure enough, after six months, Dori ran the business into the ground. Omar had borrowed $150,000 against our home, and it all ended up going to waste.

The next few years of my life were full of ups and downs. The feeling of being a mom and caring for something that was all mine gave me a sense of happiness and joy. I felt so complete having Diana in my life that I didn't care whether Omar was cheating. However, although his physical abuse didn't happen as often as before, the mental and emotional abuse continued to get worse. There wasn't a day that he didn't call me "a worthless piece of shit."

His attitude depended on whether he was high on weed or not. He was more relaxed, laidback and funny when he smoked, but without it he was short-tempered, snappy, careless and mean. He would break things around the house, especially if I refused to be intimate with him. I realized my husband was not only physically and emotionally abusive, but also addicted to alcohol, drugs and sex.

In the beginning of 1993, a dream came true for me: my grandmother moved from Pakistan to the US. It was the first time I'd seen her in fifteen years. I ran toward her with wide-open arms and a smile from ear to ear; it felt like a dream. Being in her arms after so many years, her scent and warm skin made me feel like a little girl. I felt full of love, comfort, safety, and joy. It was so soothing; I didn't want to let go. I hadn't felt like this since moving from Afghanistan. Through her I felt closer to my mom and siblings, because it wasn't too long since she had been around them. I missed my family so very much and I wanted them near me so badly.

I was so excited to show Grandma around California. I wanted to take her everywhere: shopping, entertainment, road trips and restaurants. I would bring her to my house and take care of her like a baby, even bathing her. Although she was capable of doing it herself, I enjoyed doing everything for her.

I only wished she stayed with me more often, but my uncle Asad—the one who was the former district attorney of Kabul and who used to beat me back in Germany for paying attention to my looks—didn't like her to stay with me, because he disliked my in-laws. Though they'd earned a comfortable middle-class life through owning video stores and selling cars in well-known dealerships, it bothered him that none of them had gone to college. Their money didn't matter to my uncle Asad; he only cared about status, prestige, and family name. He hated me for my marriage, which I never understood; my father and stepmom had arranged it, it's not like I had chosen it myself.

With all that in mind, Grandma was afraid of her son. Although he lived in Paris, I guess he was keeping tabs on her through the phone. She never told me this, but I knew her reasons. Otherwise she would have loved to stay with me rather than one of her two sons (my father or my other uncle).

So when she first moved, she stayed with my uncle Aziz—Uncle Asad's younger brother. I hadn't seen Uncle Asad for years—but one day, early in my grandma's stay in the US, I had a surprise encounter with him.

Unbeknownst to me, he was in town from France visiting my grandma. I showed up at my uncle Aziz's house to visit my grandma; when I walked in and greeted her, she reacted strangely—widening her eyes and putting her hand over her mouth, like she'd just seen a ghost. That's when I noticed that Uncle Asad was sitting behind her, at the table, with his back to me. I instantly froze. I had no idea what to expect from him—would he yell at me or hit me? I wasn't just concerned for myself—I was six months pregnant with my second child.

It had been about seven years since I'd seen him. But because within our culture, you have to greet your elders no matter what, I quietly said, "Hello, Uncle."

To my surprise, he turned around and greeted me cordially—even warmly. Relieved, I stepped closer to kiss his hand in customary greeting. Then he said: "I'm sorry, dear, I didn't recognize you."

That's when I realized that, when he heard me greet him, he hadn't necessarily realized it was me; it was common for young people to refer to all men of their parents' generation as 'uncle'.

Immediately, my terror returned. I took a deep breath and a step back. Then I instinctively looked around the room for an exit strategy.

Right on cue, he bellowed, "Get the hell out of here! I'm going to kill you!"

I don't remember how I got to my car, but somehow I did. I just grabbed Diana and ran. That was the last time I saw him.

When Diana was four, we planned to get pregnant again. Although my first pregnancy had been a nightmare, I thought it was time. I'd always wanted my babies to be five years apart so I could be 100% present for one child at a time, and Diana was old enough now to be in kindergarten.

I stopped taking my birth control, and sure enough, it didn't take much time for me to get pregnant. My second pregnancy didn't turn out to be any easier than my first one. As soon as I started to show, Omar started going out again partying and not coming home until three or four a.m., smelling of alcohol, weed and women's perfume, with lipstick marks on his shirts. I would wait for him night after night, worrying about what he was up to.

When he got home, if he wanted to have sex and I refused, he would kick or push me, calling me all kinds of names. Other times, he would spoon me from the back, hold one hand over my mouth and rape me. We were temporarily living in a two-bedroom apartment at that time, since our second home wasn't ready yet for us to move in. I had to stay quiet so I wouldn't wake up Diana or the neighbors next door. The next day, he would wake up and act normal, as if nothing had happened. It always depended on how hungover he was. If I said anything he didn't like hearing, he would say, "Shut your fucking mouth, your voice is annoying."

Our fights were so bad that sometimes I felt ready to just take my life so he could feel the guilt and live with it. I remember one time I even put a butcher's knife against my belly when I was nine months pregnant to show him I was ready to end my life, as well as the baby's. For me, it was all about making a memorable scene so he would stop all his bullshit, even if it cost my life. Yet no matter what I did, it didn't change his behavior.

On February 23, 1993, after 12 hours of labor, I delivered my baby girl, Marci. She was healthy and beautiful; she had fair skin and hair so light it looked bleached, but she looked just like Omar. Omar was thrilled to have another girl—especially since she looked just like his twin.

Going home from the hospital was surreal; I was now a mother of two little people who were completely dependent on me. I felt more responsible than ever. Omar was never a big help with childcare, especially when it came to night-time feedings or changing diapers. (He could have helped with both; I never breastfed my babies, since no one had ever taught me about the benefits of breast milk.)

That summer of 1993, Omar and I moved into our new home. Although our first home was over 2,400 square feet, with 4 bedrooms and 3 bathrooms, he wanted a house with a bigger backyard. That way he could build a pool and barbeque—his vision of the American dream. Our new home was 3,700 square feet with an 8,000 square foot backyard—enough space for everything he'd imagined.

Within a month of our move, one day out of the blue, he said to me: "I want to help your sister Sophia—I want to find a way to keep her here to be close to you." Omar had always had a soft spot for her, and really enjoyed doing things for her and her children. He was aware of her arranged and extremely abusive marriage, and knew how very close we were. At his best, Omar could display real generosity.

I couldn't have asked for anything more than to have my grandma and my sister together at the same time. I always envied other people that were close to their families; I could hardly remember the last time I'd had my whole family around me. I always imagine how it would be like to have both my parents with all my 4 siblings together for a day. I started to ask a thousand questions; all he said was, "I'll find a way." And he did.

The day we picked her and her two children up from the airport was one of the happiest days of my life. It was incredibly emotional for her to meet my grandma for the first time after sixteen years. There were a lot of happy and sad tears. We spent most of the day together, catching up at my uncle's house.

After a few hours, we left and went to my house. Sophia stayed with us for the first few months; the plan was to get an apartment for her, my grandma and my cousin Basin to share while we started the immigration process toward their permanent residence.

August 1996 family trip to Las Vegas with my sister Sophia

Finally, we found an apartment and moved them in. I was so excited to have all of them close by—and in the same place! But I could never have anticipated that only a day after they moved in, my whole world would come crashing down.

That day, I spent several hours helping them settle in, then went back home. Within less than nine hours of seeing them, I got a call from the one of the employees at their apartment complex. The second she reintroduced herself, I knew something was wrong. My heart was racing. I suddenly couldn't hear a thing she was saying. I kept repeating myself, asking her if my grandma was okay. I knew she was trying to tell me, but I was refusing to hear it. In a stern voice, she finally stopped me and said, "Please come now."

Omar was at work and Diana was at school, so I jumped out of bed. I didn't care what I had on. I was wearing one of Omar's T-shirts as a sleeping shirt and I didn't bother to change. I was so lost that I couldn't get myself to wash the soap out of my daughter Marci's bottle.

As I was driving toward her apartment, all I could think about was how happy and excited I had been just the night before. Having the people I loved all in one place was something I'd never had before. So far, it had been everything I'd imagined. Just the night before, Grandma had been telling us a hilarious story; she had never been so funny, imitating how my cousin Basin got drunk on his wedding night a few years back. We were all laughing so hard that tears were running down our faces.

The drive from my house to Grandma's was only ten minutes, but that ten-minute drive seemed more like ten hours. When I finally got there, I opened the door to see my sister's back facing me. She was sitting in the doorway to Grandma's room, with Grandma on her lap. At that moment, I felt paralyzed. But in seconds I was on the floor, throwing myself onto my grandmother's body. I pulled her head to my chest, shaking, begging her to get up. I hugged and kissed her cold blue body. But no matter what I did, she didn't wake up. My thoughts were blank and my legs felt weak. I couldn't believe my life had turned upside down so quickly.

Within four weeks of my grandma's passing, my sister's husband appeared from Germany all of a sudden. Ostensibly, he was there for my grandma's forty-day prayer ceremony—a ritual marking the end the mourning period. At first I didn't think anything of it. But then Omar told my sister that her husband wanted to take his son back to Germany. My sister tried to resist, and we all tried to negotiate with him, but after he talked to Omar, somehow Omar convinced us all that if my sister went back to Germany, she'd be able to have her son back. Of course, we had very little recourse; at the end of the day, we had to go along with what our husbands had decided. After a few days, her husband took his son and went back. Within a couple of weeks, my sister left for Germany, hoping to obtain custody of her son. But she never did—her husband's promises had all been lies.

Nothing was sadder than the day I dropped my sister off at the airport. We were hopeful that she'd be able to return with her son, but that never happened. She ended up moving to a women's shelter and fighting for her son. The fact that she'd let him go with his father in the first place had caused her to lose custody of him. She didn't get him back until he was seventeen years old, when his dad pulled a knife on him and he went to court to free himself from his father.

That wonderful dream of us all being together had lasted only one day. Grandma died, my sister went back to Germany, and my cousin moved back in with my uncle. Again, I was alone. It seemed that our lives were only getting worse. It was a cycle of misery, one thing after another. I was suffering not only with what I was going through with my own marriage, but also with my sister's devastation at losing her child and living in a women's shelter. I always thought about her and her safety. She told me the other women were recovering addicts or struggling with mental illness. I tried to be there for her, but the shelter had only one phone in the hallway and it wasn't easy getting hold of her.

I found myself again fighting to be strong and grateful for my girls, and doing whatever it would take to give them a world of love and peace. But I knew that wasn't possible with Omar. He wasn't the kind of a father I wanted for them.

As my responsibilities grew, so did my miseries. I constantly begged my husband to change himself for the better. He was now a grown man with kids, but he still did what he wanted to do, no matter what I said. Although he loved the idea of being a family man, he didn't act like one. He loved to spoil his children; there were no limits with him. He would come home and play with the kids after I had already bathed them, acting like everything was funny. He did anything they wanted, regardless of whether they behaved or not. He would drive to a convenience store and buy them an unlimited amount of ice cream and candy, or spend hundreds or thousands of dollars at Target on unnecessary toys or junk food.

This behavior, of course, undermined my own efforts to provide them with a sense of structure and healthy discipline. I managed to keep a set schedule for the kids when Omar was at work, but when Daddy was home it was party time, and they hardly listened to me. They knew he would just let them do whatever they wanted. I didn't believe in raising my kids without any guidelines, expectations, or discipline, or indulging them for no reason. As a parent it was very important to me for my children to learn and understand the value of things. But after Omar's shopping sprees, they always wanted new stuff a few days later. Omar had been promoted and now earned a nice income—but just because we could afford it now didn't mean that's how things should be.

In other words, we were not on the same page about how to raise our children. Worse than that, he would still fight with me, call me horrible words, and throw and break things around the house in front of his young children. I couldn't stand this; I'd witnessed my own parents fight and argue all the time, and I wanted something different for my own kids. My dad was always partying and having affairs with other women, so he was hardly around. But when he was home, it was worse; I would get so frightened when I heard or saw my parents fight. Many times we saw him beat the crap out of our mom, and at times my sister and I would cry and beg him to stop. In Germany, we witnessed him doing the same thing to our stepmom.

I also didn't want my children around tobacco, alcohol, or any type of drugs. I had bad memories of my dad and stepmom getting together with their friends every weekend to eat, drink and party. After finishing dinner, my sister and I were in charge of cleaning the table and washing the dishes. They would move to the living room and shut the door, and if they ever ran out of alcohol or cigarettes, my dad would send one of us to go to the kiosk to get it. The kiosk was walking distance from our home and was open 24/7. There were always some drunks hanging out inside, drinking and smoking. I never forgot the nasty smell.

I always said to myself that whenever I became a mom, I wanted my kids to have a very different experience from me. I wanted my babies' childhoods to be free of drama; I wanted them to only experience love in a happy, clean environment. I never believed in hitting or yelling at them. I also didn't want my kids to be around the smell of alcohol and weed.

Omar, on the other hand, would often come home high, with his eyes bloodshot red. I detested the smell of weed on his breath, his skin and his hair. If he wasn't already high, he'd go into the garage or backyard to smoke, and carry a bottle of beer with him—then come inside and hug and kiss the kids. I was horrified, afraid that one day they would be doing the same thing.

One day, to my surprise, I got a call from my father-in-law. He said he was going to Pakistan to visit his in-laws. In the meantime, he was going to hire someone to go to Afghanistan to find my mom and siblings. I repeated what he had said. I wasn't sure if I was hearing him correctly. I asked him if he was joking. My father-in-law was well known as a funny guy; his jokes always made everyone laugh. But I suspected that now he was serious. As much as I was scared of him, I also knew that he cared for me and felt bad for me. I said, "You know, this has been a lifetime dream of mine."

He said, "I know, and that's why I'm telling you that I'll find her." I was so stunned that I just started to cry.

I felt both excited and scared. I was worried that my mom and siblings could be dead. My sister and I hadn't heard from them for over five years; the war with Russia was still in full swing, and we'd lost contact with them. I thought if they were dead, God forbid, I would rather not know—but if they were alive I wanted to have them in my life. As the weeks went on, the curiosity was killing me. I couldn't sleep, tossing and turning every night. I kept thinking about how wonderful it would be to see my mother and my younger siblings after seventeen years.

Finally, after about 4 weeks, my father-in-law called me from Pakistan, saying there was someone that would like to talk to me. When I heard him say that, my heart skipped a beat. I didn't know what to expect.

I heard a lady's voice calling me, "My deer." When I was young, my mom had always said I looked like a deer because of my large eyes.

Those same eyes suddenly filled with tears of happiness and relief. I screamed, "Mom? Mom, is that you?"

She replied, "Yes my daughter, it's me, your mother."

It felt like a dream. She was on the other end of the phone with me. The whole time, I was thinking about how I wished my sister was there to talk to her too. I couldn't wait to tell her. I couldn't believe I was actually talking to my own mom. It didn't feel real.

I couldn't wait to call my sister to share the great news with her. Once she answered her phone, I said, "Sophia, Mom and them are alive! They're alive!"

She couldn't understand me clearly because I couldn't contain my excitement. She said, "Why are you screaming? What are you saying? Why don't you calm down first then tell me what's going on."

Then she finally understood what I shared with her, and we both cried our hearts out. For once, our tears were ones of relief and joy. We talked for a while. I told her what our plans were and that I would keep her posted.

After a couple of weeks, Omar left for Pakistan. We agreed it made more sense for him to go first and get them situated, then return to the US before I went. Diana was in kindergarten and was too obsessed with school for me to let her miss it.

In August 1993, I left for Pakistan with Marci, who was six months old at the time. Diana stayed with Omar and our live-in nanny, Rosie, who we'd recently hired to help out around the house.

Omar thought four weeks would be long enough for my trip, but I wanted to go for at least three months. He told me, "You won't last there for more than a week. I know what it's like there—you're not going to feel safe and comfortable."

We argued about it and settled on a compromise of two months. I was so happy; I was counting down the days, hours, and minutes until I left. It seemed like time was going so slowly—even slower as my departure approached. Once I arrived, the airport in Pakistan seemed small, messy and dirty to me. People were pushing each other to get to their bags. After managing to get my bags, I found my way outside the airport.

As I looked around, what I saw was complete chaos. There were cars everywhere in every direction honking at each other; people were walking in all directions, trash was strewn across the streets, and everywhere I looked I saw nothing but a big mess. I also felt scared, thinking, *If someone kidnapped me and my baby girl, there would be no questions asked. How could anyone know of our whereabouts?* It just seemed like there were no laws. All of this was not too far off from what I had imagined; it reminded me a little of what I remembered of Afghanistan. Still, it was a shock to my system.

I finally saw my brother waving his arms to get my attention. I started walking toward him with my bags in a cart. I greeted my brother with big hugs and tears. I asked where everyone else was. He said, "They're all waiting for you eagerly at home."

The 30-minute drive from the airport to my mom's was both sad and amazing; I couldn't believe what my eyes were seeing. I saw things that broke my heart, like people living in mud homes with traffic and people swirling around them. Nothing felt safe or clean. I suddenly knew what Omar had tried to warn me about. I tried to calm myself down and focus on seeing my family.

As we pulled in, my brother said, "Okay, we are home." I immediately opened the door and ran toward the front gate. I yelled to my brother to bring Marci with him.

The next thing I felt was a drop of water on my face. I was totally disoriented; I thought I was asleep and maybe my kids were splashing me with their bottle of milk. I didn't know where I was. I heard a woman's crying voice caressing my face and talking to me. I was hearing her calling me her beautiful deer and saying how much she missed me. I slowly opened my eyes, wondering what was going on.

I became instantly aware that I was in my mom's arms. When I tried to pull my head up, I felt this massive pain on my forehead. I realized that, in my haste to get inside, I must have hit my head on the front gate and passed out.

My mom's scent was exactly the way I remembered. I couldn't believe how real that moment was. For so many years I had prayed and hoped for this day, and it was a dream come true. I couldn't hold back my tears. I started to sob like a lost child in the middle of a desert.

My three siblings were all grown up. Maria was now 21 years old, married and a mom to her 6-month-old son, Salomon. My two brothers—Froch, 19, and Yama, 18— were so grown up. How I remembered them as little kids; they all looked so different now. After hours of hugging, kissing and chatting with every single one of them, we still had so much to catch up on.

After spending some time with my family, I realized that my brother Froch was kind of shy and not very talkative. He seemed very quiet, but super sweet and attentive. I wasn't quite sure why he was different compared to my brother Yama and sister Maria.

Maria had dinner ready. We ate the traditional way, sitting around a tablecloth on the floor, with four different kinds of dishes. I hadn't experienced this since I left Afghanistan, and it felt comforting.

The next day, I was sleeping in the same room as my mom and both my brothers. As I was asleep, I heard my brother Yama calling out to my older brother Froch, "Hey crazy, get up! You have to go to the bakery and get some bread." Froch got out of bed and went quietly to the bathroom. Without saying a word, he quickly washed up and left. It broke my heart how he was being treated. I didn't understand why they called him "crazy"—but then I remembered how my mom used to call him crazy when he was little too. I realized that when I left Afghanistan, my mom had never stopped being mean to him, making the younger siblings treat him the same way. That made me very sad, and also upset with my mom.

The more time went by, the more deeply I understood the differences between mine and my siblings' upbringings. Although my sister Sophia and I had missed out on a whole lot of life growing up in Germany, we were never allowed to call each other bad names. Our stepmom had made sure of that. In the early days, whenever she heard us saying anything bad to each other, not only would we get in trouble, but she would also lecture us for hours. Sometimes she would start lecturing at the breakfast table and wouldn't stop until almost dinner time. We had hated those lectures. Now, looking back, I saw that some were a complete waste of time, while others had been beneficial.

Being with my family, I envied the bond they had with each other. I felt like an outsider in a sense, and it made me a little uneasy. I would never wish to be in their shoes; seeing the way they lived and hearing their horrific stories about constantly moving and surviving the seventeen years of war was heartbreaking. But being here with my mother, now a mom myself, I was suddenly questioning her parenting. What made me the most upset with my mom was her not putting her family first and being unwilling to move to Germany with us. We could have all had such a great life growing up together, with so many shared memories. Now what we had was missed opportunities. I blamed what I saw as my mom's selfishness.

As more days went by, my anger grew. I was questioning everything. *Why did my father leave the rest of his family behind? Why was my mother okay with separating her children like that? What kind of a mom would do that?* Being a mom now, I could never see myself splitting up my children. As much as I loved my mother, I was now questioning her love for us. I started to have mixed emotions about her. It was killing me inside, and I felt like I couldn't tell anyone what I was feeling. Overall, I was just confused, with so many unanswered questions.

In the meantime, my baby Marci started to get sick on our second day there. Her vomiting and diarrhea were nonstop. I thought it would get better, but over time it just kept getting worse. She couldn't hold down anything I gave her to eat and drink. Within a minute or so, she'd vomit it back up. I finally told my brother that I had to take her to a doctor. My family agreed, and we took her to a local doctor.

The doctor told me to stop feeding her baby food and to simply feed her crackers with plain rice and water. But no matter what I did, she didn't get better. I finally told my brother that I had to take her to an American doctor or hospital. I didn't trust any of the other local doctors.

Once I arrived at the hospital emergency room, everything looked familiar. It was very much like home, and it made me feel comfortable that my baby girl was now in good hands. Yet despite that feeling, nothing they did helped heal her. We were now on our fifth day, and Marci was still unable to hold down food or fluids. When Omar called me, I told him how sick Marci was and that I hadn't been able to enjoy my stay because of worrying about her. I told him that I needed to come home as soon as possible. At this point, I was scared for her life.

Omar couldn't believe that I was ready to come home this soon. He told me he was going to check out some flights and would let me know. Marci's sickness wasn't improving and she was getting more and more fragile. I was horrified. *What if I lost her?*

Omar called me the next day and said he'd found us a flight in a couple of days. I couldn't wait to get back and take her to her own doctor. At the same time, I was sad that my entire ten days had gone by just taking care of Marci. I'd hardly had the opportunity to spend quality time with my family, but I knew I had no choice. I had to leave as soon as possible so that I could save my daughter's health.

On my last day, I asked my brother to take me to the flea market so I could get some souvenirs. As I reached the street shops, Maria started to look at some items while I had my brother record some videos for me. When one store owner noticed my brother recording, he started yelling and called us all kinds of names. He said, "I'm gonna kill you guys!" and pointed his revolver right at us.

My heart was racing like never before. My brother immediately yelled, "Run! Just run as fast as you can!" I quickly looked at him with fear and then took off. As I ran, my flip flops came off my feet and I started running barefoot. It was a very hot humid day and must have been over 100 degrees. It felt like a burning fire under my feet, but I kept running. All I was thinking about was, *What's going to happen to my baby girl Marci? And my Diana at home!* I couldn't bear the thought of my girls not having me in their lives. That thought kept me going.

I couldn't hear the guy yelling anymore, but we kept running until we couldn't run any longer. When I turned back, we noticed he was gone. I couldn't believe what had just happened. We could have been killed. I was in shock. It made me realize how fragile life can be. I thought to myself, *I knew from day one that I didn't feel safe here.* That experience was the last straw for me. I just couldn't wait to get on the plane and go home.

Saying goodbye to my family the next day was one of the hardest things I'd ever had to do. We were all crying with the grief of being separated once again. I'd barely gotten to spend any time with all of them. It seemed like I'd just gotten there, and now I was already saying my goodbyes. I promised them all that I would come back without my baby girl.

Marci was still sick, so my flight back home was not very pleasant. She kept on having diarrhea nonstop and ran through multiple diapers in a 12-hour flight. It was very frustrating, but I somehow managed to take care of her. She was very weak and fragile. No matter what I was giving her, she still couldn't hold anything in. I just wanted to get her home so I could take her to her doctor.

The second Marci saw her dad, she started to smile and threw herself into Omar's arms. The first thing I did was give her some water. After that, I had Omar bring Marci some Gerber baby food; she ate three bottles and was finally able to hold it down without any vomit or diarrhea, for the first time in ten days. It was interesting how quickly she healed. It seemed like nothing was wrong with her anymore.

The next day, we took her to the doctor. As soon as the doctor saw her, she said, "Take her to the hospital ASAP. She is extremely dehydrated. If you'd waited even a few more hours, she might not have survived." As scared I was, I couldn't be any happier that we were back. Marci ended up being in the hospital for three days before she was released. When she came home, she was back to her happy self, smiling and playing with her sister Diana.

When things settled, I had some time to think about my family in Pakistan, and about all the horrible things they had endured for over seventeen years of war. They had watched neighbors lose their lives in bombings and rocket shootings. They'd been forced to move from place to place.

The worst story of all for me was how my brother-in-law had married my sister, Maria. Maria, being almost three years younger than me, had married her husband at the age of eighteen. She was drop-dead gorgeous; I had always heard people say I was the most beautiful girl in our family, but when I met Maria for the first time after seventeen years, I thought she was the most beautiful woman I had ever seen. Her skin was smooth and flawless. I had to admit it made me a little jealous, but in a good way. I had never felt this way about anyone.

Her husband was a sergeant and fourteen years older than her. He'd apparently seen her in the market, followed her, and left. A few days later, he went to my mom and asked her for Maria's hand. My mom and Maria refused. Maria didn't want to be married to a sergeant, knowing the situation. She knew he wouldn't have a long life, and she was not attracted to him.

When Maria and my mom refused to accept the sergeant's proposal more than once, he couldn't take the refusal. On his third try, he pulled his gun, held it to her forehead and screamed, "If you say no to me one more time, I'm going to shoot her right now. You're mine and we are going to get married!" And that's how he married her: at gunpoint.

My heart was aching for them. I wasn't satisfied with my visit. I wanted to go back. I just didn't know how to make it happen anytime soon. Marci was so young I didn't feel comfortable leaving her with our nanny Rosie.

My marriage still had its ups and downs, and the downs were no better than before. Almost every day, my husband would say to me, "You worthless piece of shit, look at yourself in the mirror, you cunt." I thought every day about leaving him, but especially now that he had helped me with my family, I felt obligated and also stuck financially. I had nowhere to go. Every day, I woke up and told myself, *it'll be a better day tomorrow.*

One thing that really helped me keep going was working out on a daily basis. No matter how hectic my days were, I would always find a way to make time for the gym, five days a week. That helped me not only stay in shape, but it kept me sane.

In the summer of 1994, we invited my sister Sophia to come visit again. This time she was without her son, since she'd lost custody of him to his father. It was bittersweet seeing her. She always gave me a sense of love and comfort. I had made a couple of awesome friends through beauty school, Dina and Nicole; we all became very close and to this day they're like sisters to me. But Sophia was someone I had shared all my sorrows with. We knew each other's pain and all the misery we'd gone through in life.

Prior to her arrival, I told Omar that I was no longer going to allow him to control my freedom. I told him, "I'm now twenty-five years old, and I can decide for myself where to go and what I want to do. You're not my father, nor are you God to take my freedom away. You're only my husband, and I never had a chance to do anything alone with my sister." He didn't say a word in response.

So when Sophia arrived on her first day, I told her that I had gotten my freedom from Omar, and in order for me to prove it to him, we had to go out until really late. As much as she begged me and told me how tired she was, I wasn't taking no for an answer. After we got home from the airport, I let her shower and rest for a little, and then I took her out to Laguna Beach. We had a great time alone with no parents, siblings, husbands or kids. We were talking to strangers and laughing; it was so much fun just to go out and meet people. It was a perfect night that I didn't want to end.

The next day, Omar called me from work. He called me all kinds of names as usual, and accused me of cheating because I'd gotten home later than he expected. Knowing that I hadn't done anything wrong, only enjoy an evening with my sister, it upset me that he'd accused me of something

I didn't do. I told him, "If that's what you think of me, then it's best we divorce."

His response was, "I don't give a damn. If you want a divorce, then go ahead. No one's stopping you."

He would say this to me every time I mentioned divorce to him, so I realized maybe that was what he wanted too. I already knew the marriage wasn't going anywhere. He wasn't changing anyway, so why suffer?

So, I hired an attorney. I paid $500 down to file for divorce. This was my second attempt.

When I told Omar what I'd done, he freaked out and started to apologize for his behavior. He cried and begged, but I stayed firm with my decision. Unfortunately, that didn't last long. He kept begging, and even had his family come and talk to me. This went on for weeks; in the meantime, he was on his best behavior. It made me change my mind and drop the divorce.

After a long talk about how I wanted him to be as a husband and father, he agreed to everything I said. For a moment, I was happy. I thought it was going to be different now.

That night he wanted to be intimate. I told him, "I've been off my pills for almost a month now." As with the last time I'd filed for divorce, I had immediately stopped taking my birth control pills. I hated taking them; I really cared about health, and knew that in the long run it wasn't good for my body. He said, "Don't worry, I'll be careful again," and I trusted him.

A few weeks later, I didn't get my period. I freaked out and scheduled an appointment to see my gynecologist. He tested me for pregnancy, and it came out positive. My heart sank. I just wanted to shoot Omar. I couldn't believe he'd lied to me. Although I'd quickly gone back to taking my birth control pills when we were together again, I guess it had been too late.

When I told him about the pregnancy, he had a big smile on his face right away. He told me, "I am so excited for us. Hopefully, now we can have a boy." He seemed like he had it all planned out.

I couldn't bear the idea of having another kid with him and going through what I'd gone through with my other two pregnancies. I was now even more angry and frustrated. I didn't know what to do next. I knew an abortion wasn't an option; I still regretted my first one. I felt like he'd gotten me this time. I couldn't raise three kids on my own, and knowing him, the positive changes would only last a month or so.

I started questioning what to do. It was even harder to leave now. Where would I go with three small children if he started to act as he had during my other two pregnancies? I felt overwhelmed, scared, and stuck. My family in Pakistan needed our financial help, since the war still prevented them from going back to Afghanistan. It would be impossible for me to do much for them on my own; I didn't have a job, and had almost no work experience.

My first trimester was very emotional. All I did was eat badly and continue to get bigger. Again, Omar started to call me Penguin, which I hated. Thankfully, this time around, he wasn't as physically abusive. But the mental abuse never stopped.

In my second trimester, I told him that I wanted to go back to see my family again, but this time without Marci.

We still had our nanny, Rosie, living with us, and Marci was very attached to her by now. So, I felt comfortable leaving her.

At first, Omar was a little shocked that I wanted to go while pregnant, but I told him, "If I don't go now, then once our baby is born, it'll be impossible to go." So he agreed and sent me back to Pakistan.

This time I only wanted to go for three weeks. My arrival was a little easier this time without Marci. Pakistan hadn't changed, and my family was very excited to see me again. This time, I was very calm and relaxed. I was able to spend quality time with all of my three siblings and my mother. I learned that my brothers and sister didn't have much knowledge or education about anything except about the eighteen years of war they had experienced and the losses they had endured.

I couldn't hold back my tears, knowing what these poor kids had been through. I'd thought I had it hard, but at least I'd had a safe home and material comforts. When I asked my mom why her kids hadn't gone to school, she started to cry and asked, "What school?" She said that almost every day the schools would get bombarded. She was always hearing about someone's child dying in a bombing—or little boys and girls would simply disappear, and their parents would never find them. They had no legal recourse.

She also mentioned that on many occasions, strangers would break into her home in the middle of the night, looking for my young brothers to kidnap so they could train them to be fighters or use them for sex. She used to have my brothers jump or climb high walls to the neighbor's house for their safety. Several times they were caught sleeping, but my mom begged the men not to take her sons away. She lied and said that her husband had died in the war and told them that the only men she had left in her life were her young boys. Mercifully, this worked. Still, the family was forced to move often; at times they would leave their house in the middle of the night, crawling through the streets to her brother's house to try and find sanctuary—but truly, nowhere was safe.

It broke my heart to hear how they'd suffered. But I still couldn't understand why my mother hadn't come to Germany from the start. It continued to bother me and anger me. I finally started to question my mom, and her response was, "Your father had me in his passport as his cousin and our kids as his cousins' kids."

Now, what my father did wasn't right, but I still didn't understand why my mother would separate her children. As a mother now, I felt I would do whatever it took to make sure my babies could all be together, and that none of my kids would be raised by another woman. It really made me question my mother's love for all of her five children.

After endless conversations with her, I came to understand that she hadn't trusted her husband, nor the idea of moving to a strange country she'd never been to. My mother had never traveled by plane before. She'd never left Afghanistan, and she didn't know much about Germany's laws. In Afghanistan, if you get a divorce, the kids go automatically to their father—no questions asked. And there were no laws protecting women against domestic violence. Women get physically and mentally abused in all kinds of ways by their husbands and in-laws, and it's perfectly acceptable according to Afghan law. There's nothing a woman can do or say to save herself from abuse. She feared that in Germany, the situation would be the same or even worse.

Even with all this, I didn't understand her decision to not join the rest of her family. I felt that the only way my babies could be taken away from me was over my dead body. I couldn't help but feel that, though my mother and I might have the same blood, we didn't have the same type of love and care for our children. It changed the way I loved and respected her. But certainly she has paid her dues many times over. I always wondered if she ever regretted her decision, knowing now how her five kids suffered in almost every possible way.

My last night in Pakistan was extremely hard. As I was packing, we were all crying and wishing that my family could board the flight with me. One of my brothers grabbed my hairbrush, took a few pieces of hair from the bristles and said, "I'm going to carry it with me everywhere I go. This will be a constant reminder that you're with me at all times." My tears immediately started falling like heavy rain. I held him in my arms so hard, I didn't want to let him go.

I promised them all that I would do whatever it took to help them to move to America. I knew it would be many years before I could make it happen, but thought it would be something for them to look forward to. It was obvious that Pakistan didn't offer them much, with its corrupt police and horrible living conditions.

When I arrived home, I was pleased that Rosie had kept the house very neat and clean, just the way I preferred. Everything seemed normal and like I hadn't left. The next day when we woke up, Omar went to work, and I dropped off Diana at school.

Later in the day, I noticed that a few things weren't in place. One of my candle holders was missing. I didn't know what to think of it, so I didn't bother to ask Rosie. I thought she might have broken it while cleaning and didn't want to put her on the spot since she hadn't mentioned it. Then I noticed my tea kettle was chipped. Now, I started to look at things around the house to see if anything else was out of the ordinary. I had a set of candle holders with candles in them on a shelf over my dining table. I noticed those were also burned, which was strange because they were meant to be decor and never used.

I started to get suspicious that something had happened between Omar and Rosie. I pictured them having a romantic candlelit night and then a fight in which they threw objects around the house. Knowing my husband, it wouldn't surprise me if he'd had sex with our nanny. But to my own surprise, I didn't feel jealous or threatened. I wasn't sure why I had felt those things in the past. Sometimes he would flirt with someone just to get a reaction out of me. I guess that was his way of killing my self-esteem.

I almost wanted him to like Rosie so he could let me go, but that wasn't the case. He'd been nicer to me than he had during my other two pregnancies. I wondered, *is it because we found out we are finally having a boy, or because I am more confident in my skin?* One way or another, I still wanted to confront him. I knew I would accept any explanation he gave me. What other choice did I have? There was nothing I could do, even if he admitted it to me.

I spent my entire day imagining everything that I thought had happened and planning how I was going to ask him. When he got home from work that night, I asked him very casually, "Do you know anything about the burned candles? Or the chipped tea kettle?"

He said, "What are you talking about? What candles? What candle holder? I have no idea, babe!" He paused and continued, "Why are you asking me? Why don't you ask Rosie?" That was all he said before he changed the subject, "How was your day with the girls?"

Although I knew the answer he was avoiding, I had to ask just to get it out of my system. Somehow I managed to stash my suspicions away, and told myself I would deal with it some other time.

I thought about asking Rosie several times, but I finally decided to not question her. I needed her in my life. She was a really good nanny: young, pretty, loving and clean. It was fun to talk to her and be around her. A few times, I'd even taken her out and had Omar watch the kids. Finding the right nanny was a big challenge, and I had a hard time trusting people with my kids. So, I simply forgave her without her even knowing I'd suspected anything.

As I got bigger from my pregnancy, so did my appetite. My appetite was much bigger this time. Omar's fat jokes also kept getting funnier…according to him. Meanwhile, I felt terrible. Taking care of my girls and getting bigger was very hard for me. I just wanted to press fast forward and get to the part where I could hold my baby boy. I had always wanted an older brother. Now, I was having my dream little man, and I was so ready. I wanted to love him and raise him to know that he could do anything he dreamed of.

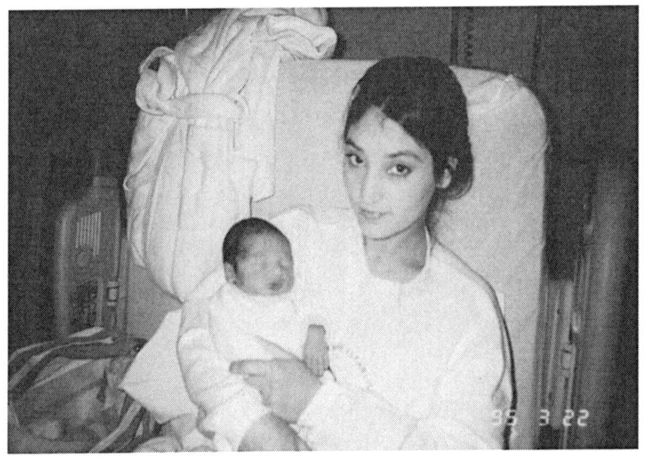

March 1995 in hospital with my first son, Edriz

Edriz was born on March 21, 1995. The Star of the World was his nickname from birth, and I still call him that today. The day he was born, I was ecstatic. I had never felt such fulfillment in my entire life. My heart felt so full and I couldn't stop smiling. I felt so proud, and in a weird way suddenly worthy: in our culture, having a son is a big deal. He was the handsomest baby boy I had ever seen.

The next day, we went home. Rosie had been taking care of the girls while I was in the hospital, and Omar took a few days off work to be with us. When we got home, the house was sparkling and neat. Rosie knew exactly how much I loved a clean house. The next three days, Edriz and I stayed upstairs in my bedroom with a bassinet for him right next to my bed. I couldn't wait for him to start using his own room. The nursery was beautifully done, with an animal/forest theme, but I always felt more comfortable keeping my newborn next to me for at least the first three months.

After a couple of days resting upstairs in my room, I was ready to go downstairs. I came down and laid on the couch in our family room. I wanted to see my girls once they came back from school. As I stepped into the family room, I saw Rosie in the kitchen cleaning the countertops. Omar had just walked in from the backyard and came to see Edriz. He chatted with him for a few minutes until I noticed that Edriz had dirtied his diaper. I asked Omar if he could get me a diaper from upstairs, since it was still hard for me to walk and move around. He looked at me and said, "Why don't you get it yourself?"

I said, "Really? Is that a question? Don't you know why I can't get it myself?"

He replied, "I don't care. I'm not your maid, you fucking bitch. Go get it yourself!"

As soon as he said that, he went into the backyard and shut the door behind him. I just couldn't believe where all that was coming from. Just because I asked him to bring a diaper, I got this response? I thought if anything, he would be very happy and excited that we had our boy now. At that moment, I lost control.

I looked over at Rosie. Her head was down as she wiped the counters; it seemed like she wasn't going to acknowledge anything that had just happened. I put Edriz down, went to the kitchen to grab a big knife and ran to the backyard, looking for Omar. As soon as I went outside, I screamed at the top of my lungs. All I wanted to do was hurt him. I wanted to stab him until he begged me to let him go. He needed to know how much I was losing it. I was shocked at myself, but I couldn't seem to get it together.

Omar was hiding, and I couldn't find him anywhere. I needed to get my anger out, so I started to stab the patio leg over and over. I stabbed it fifty times, and at one point I cut my own fingers and hand without feeling a thing. I was still screaming and cursing at him. At some point, I got tired and stopped.

I went back inside, realized all the blood I had on me, and cleaned myself up. My throat felt very dry and itchy, and I hardly had any voice left. I grabbed Edriz and went back into my room. I locked the door and cried myself to sleep with Edriz next to me. A couple of hours later, I woke up to Edriz crying and realized I had to feed him. I knew my life wasn't going to change, even if I had ten kids with Omar. He only got me pregnant so he could keep me stuck. I really felt like I had no choice but to stay.

Little did I know that the attitude he gave me that day was a performance for Rosie; he wanted to show her that he didn't give a damn about what I asked of him. Years later, I found out he'd had a full-on sexual relationship with her during the three years she lived with us. Omar was a very sex-driven guy. He wanted sex every single night, even though he could only last less than a minute. If I refused him, he would punch holes in the walls, throw things around or slam the doors so hard the kids would wake up. I guess he couldn't resist taking advantage of the opportunity to have sex with the other woman in the house.

Ever since re-establishing contact with my family in Pakistan, we had been working very hard to get them safely to the US. Finally, we arranged a visa for my mother.

Meanwhile, as we prepared for my mom's arrival, I continued to struggle in my marriage. As a mother of three, all my days would start at eight a.m. and last until midnight. It wasn't easy for me to feed all my babies at the same time, bathe them, get them ready for bed, read to them and call it a night. After I was done with my girls, it was Edriz's turn. Afterwards, I would make sure I cleaned everything for the next day. Rosie would go to her room around nine p.m. and I would just wait for Omar to come home.

At this point, Omar had a higher position at work as a finance manager; therefore, a lot of nights he wouldn't get home until 11:00 p.m. Some nights, when he got home, he would wake up the babies and bring them downstairs to play with them. I never understood that. Didn't he know how long it took me to put them all to bed and how strict I was when it came to my kids' schedule? In the end, I was the one putting them back to sleep—and it was never easy, they would be cranky and tired. All I wanted at the end of my day was to have an hour or so to myself to just sit and watch some news and relax.

The mornings were even worse: the minute he woke up, he'd go wake the kids up and take them to his cousin's house down the street to get high and have his coffee without changing their diapers, dressing them or feeding them. My kids would be playing barefoot with their saggy diapers around him in the backyard while he was getting high with his cousin. Almost every morning when I got out of bed, no one would be home. That would make me extremely upset because it messed up the daily schedule I had for my babies. It caused us to fight, and every time he ended the fight the same way: "Go eat shit, you worthless piece of shit, you cunt."

Worst of all, his drug use had escalated—it wasn't just weed anymore. The very first time he offered me drugs was New Year's Eve, 1996. He and a couple of his work buddies, along with their wives, had rented a limo for all of us to drive down to Beverly Hills for a party. During our drive, one of his friends took a little Ziploc bag out of his pocket and start putting it on a little clear tray, crushing it and prepping it in perfect little lines. It looked like a movie scene to me; I'd never experienced anything like that in my entire life. I looked at Karen, one of the other guys' wives; she just looked back at me with a soft smile and said, "It's okay, Laila—it's New Year's Eve."

After they all snorted some, Karen pushed the tray my way. I pushed it back and looked at Omar with disappointment. He refused to meet my gaze. Again, Karen said, "Laila, try it!"

But no matter how many times I pushed it back, they all gave me this look—like if I didn't do it, the party would be ruined. I said to Karen, "This isn't me. We both have kids— how can we do this? What if I die?"

She said, "I promise you won't die."

Then I told her, "I don't know how to do it."

She said, "I'll teach you!" and she did.

I eventually succumbed to their pressure and did it—but as I snorted, I tried to blow out at the same time so that as little as possible would go into my nose. After that, I told them, "I'm good."

I actually never felt anything, which was a huge relief for me. Deep down, I couldn't wait to get home and have a fight with Omar. But by the time I got ready for bed, I realized Omar had already passed out.

When Edriz was one year old, Marci three and Diana eight, I started feeling desperate again. I knew that if I stayed with him any longer, pretty soon my kids would understand exactly what their father was up to. My worst nightmare was that if I didn't leave him, maybe someday my kids would be doing exactly what he was doing: just smoking weed and selling cars. That was the last thing I wanted for my kids' future, knowing that we as parents are our children's role models.

I had given him a lot of chances to change, so we could have a better, happy life. But nothing I said seemed to motivate him to change in any way. He told me, "There's nothing you can do or say to change me. Not unless I want to!"

How true this was. But it didn't fully sink in until I heard it from Oprah, of all people.

I used to adore Oprah; I looked up to her so much. I used to call her my TV mom. I watched her show religiously while cleaning during my kids' daily naptime at 3:00 p.m. I was riveted by a series of shows she aired in which she helped reunite people with lost loved ones—I daydreamed about contacting her so she could help me permanently reunite with my family.

That day, the subject of the show was divorce. She had couples who had ended up staying in their marriage for their kids' sake; then she had a group of parents who'd all divorced. Surprisingly, the kids of the parents who'd stayed together ended up in a very unhappy marriages, while the children of the divorced couples had happy lives with their spouses. Oprah also interviewed marriage counselors and marriage therapists, who confirmed that staying in an unhappy marriage for the kids' sake was a big mistake; it only resulted in kids thinking their parents' unhappy marriage was normal, thereby dooming them to the same cycle. She also talked about how you can't change your partner unless they're willing to change.

Oprah may not know this, but she changed my life. The resonances with my own situation were obvious. It suddenly became clear to me that I needed to stop trying to change Omar. If I already knew he wouldn't change for me or for our children, why was I wasting my life with him? In the summer of 1996, I decided to file for divorce again. I wanted to raise the kids on my own; I wanted Omar out of our lives for good. This was my third time filing since I had been married.

In the end, this third attempt didn't work out. The same thing happened that had happened before: Omar would beg and promise to change, and he'd have his family come meet with me. They'd say that this time was different because he didn't want to lose his kids, that he was ready to do whatever it took to save his marriage, that I should give him one last chance. After a month or so, I'd get back together with him for the sake of my kids.

Plus, I knew that my mom's move from Pakistan was very close; I didn't like the idea of her arriving while I was going through a divorce. When Omar went to Pakistan, he had apparently built a close relationship with her; at the time, of course, she had no idea of the hurdles I'd faced in my marriage. Even when she did find out, it wasn't a big deal to her; her response was, "No relationship is perfect; just have patience and things will get easier."

I also knew she was worried about her kids. Omar and I were supporting them financially. Therefore, I believe that my mom's advice wasn't really given with my best interest in mind; it was obvious she was worried about her family's continuing survival. She didn't have much faith in my ability to work and be successful; her doubt that I could make it on my own financially didn't help at all.

When I canceled my third attempt at divorce, I tried to communicate with Omar that if we were going to stay together, we really needed to focus on each other by getting to know each other, since our arranged marriage hadn't given us that chance. I also told him he needed to stop pressuring me to have sex whenever he wanted to. Of course, he agreed—it was in his interest at that moment to tell me what I wanted to hear. But Omar wasn't anywhere near close to understanding what kind of communication I needed, nor what really made me happy.

August 1995 with my friends. Nicole on the left and Dina on the right of me.

My mother arrived in February 1996. It was wonderful to have her with us. Omar was very happy; he felt a sense of accomplishment, since he was the one who had filed and finished all her paperwork to get her visa. He also liked that my mom was only in her late forties—still young and healthy enough to babysit for us whenever he wanted to go places. I never left my babies with anyone unless they were sleeping for the rest of the night; otherwise, I would just stay home. It was nice knowing that my babies were in good hands with my mom, and she really enjoyed watching and taking care of them. For the first time as a mom, I could actually leave my house without being worried about my kids.

But, as always, it seemed that when one door opened for the better, another shut for the worse. My father and stepmother had decided to move out of the US just about a week before my mother's arrival. It seemed to me that my stepmom didn't like the idea of my mom living in the US. I never heard from them after their move, nor was I even allowed to know where they'd gone. That was very painful for me: it felt like I was gaining my mother but now losing the other half of my family.

As hard as I'd tried to bring my family together, I had simply failed. I missed my younger siblings terribly. After all, I had raised them—they were my first babies. Now I'd lost them, without even knowing where they'd moved. I always thought once I had my mom with me, the void of motherhood in my life would be fulfilled—but I was now feeling the void of losing the family I'd known and grown up with. Every time I tried somehow to find their contact information from some of the relatives, I always got the cold shoulder. I ran around in circles until it became obvious that I wasn't allowed to contact them, and I finally gave up.

A few years later, they started to come back for visits; my in-laws would tell me they'd invited my family for dinner, but I wouldn't be invited. It was clear to them that if I was there, my dad and stepmom would not come. Every time my in-laws apologized for not inviting me, my eyes would instantly get watery; at times I would just burst into tears. I was dying to see my siblings, knowing that they were only a ten-minute drive from me. It felt like I was being punished for helping to save my mom and siblings from the Taliban's. control. I wouldn't see anyone from that side of the family for another ten years, when my sister came for a surprise visit.

Omar and I now had a little more freedom to do things as a couple, but no matter what we did, it always turned into a fight. Sometimes I would try to ignore the hurtful things he said, but then there would be times that I just couldn't hold in my anger and I would defend myself. Though these fights always intruded on our dates, he somehow always managed to bring me down afterwards. He would touch me playfully and joke around until I cracked a smile. He could suddenly become very charming: looking at me with his green eyes, his thick eyebrows raised in a guilty look, a smirk on his full lips. I couldn't deny that he was handsome; sometimes his good looks made it a lot easier for me to ignore the situation and make the best out of our day.

Whenever I agreed to give him another chance, he immediately wanted to have sex—and this time, after I canceled the third divorce attempt, was no different. He argued that he hadn't been with me for over a month now and couldn't wait any longer. But it was a huge turnoff to me, since it made me feel like I was back in the same miserable life in which my needs and preferences meant nothing next to his.

Once again, I'd gone off my birth control pills after filing for divorce—and despite his promises, I once again found myself pregnant almost immediately. I started feeling sick in the mornings; at first I thought maybe it was food poisoning, but after a few days of nausea, I took a pregnancy test. I was extremely upset with myself: how stupid was I, to find myself back in this situation? How the hell did I go back to trusting this awful man again and again?

I never wanted to terminate another pregnancy, since I'd always regretted my first termination. But I just couldn't imagine going through with this one. After hours of crying,

I called Omar at work and told him that since he'd gotten me pregnant without my consent, I was going to terminate the pregnancy.

He was blown away when I told him about my pregnancy; immediately, the tone of his voice changed, and all I could hear was excitement. He kept saying how much he loved me and how happy he was and how much he hoped it would be another boy so we could have two of each. Disgusted, I told him, "Keep on dreaming—I'm not going to keep it, period!" and hung up the phone. He tried calling back over and over, but I didn't care to talk to him anymore. I called my gynecologist and scheduled a termination.

When Omar got home that night, he was ecstatic from joy and tried to be very loving. I told him I'd made an appointment to terminate the pregnancy. He was in disbelief; he didn't think that I would be brave enough to go through with the abortion, since I was pretty traumatized from my first one. But I didn't see any other option.

My mom was also very excited when I told her about the pregnancy. When I told her about the termination, she started to cry and begged me not to do it. She considered the pregnancy to be a blessing and thought that if I rejected God's blessing, our family would be punished. No matter how much she and Omar talked to me and begged me to keep it, I was firm about my abortion. I couldn't see it any other way. I knew my marriage would end at some point, and I couldn't imagine being alone with four kids.

As we left the house for the appointment, my mother again begged and cried for me to stop; the whole drive there, Omar was begging and trying to change my mind. But I was determined and there was no chance of turning back. I wanted to show Omar that he couldn't control me or my life any more.

We walked into the doctor's office, signed in and paid my $100 copay, and then I got seated to be called for my procedure. As I waited anxiously, with a cluttered brain and my heart in my stomach, I became even more upset and angry at Omar. Everything I was going through right now was because of him; if he wasn't the way he was, then maybe I'd be happy and want to keep this child inside of me. These voices in my head were driving me crazy. I just wanted them to call me already so I could get it over with.

They finally called my name. I got up and gave Omar a long hard look. I wanted him to know that this was all his fault. He wanted to come with me, but the nurse said he wasn't allowed to. I followed her into the procedure room; after she checked my blood pressure, she asked me to change into a blue hospital gown. Then she left the room and said the doctor would be with me shortly.

At this point, my body simply felt frozen. I couldn't even move my fingers down my boot to open the zipper. After about ten minutes, the doctor walked into the room. I still hadn't undressed. It must have been obvious how upset I was. I quickly looked up and said, "I'm sorry, doctor."

He said, "No worries, honey, take your time—I'll come back in a few minutes." Then he shut the door and left.

I just sat there; I still couldn't bring myself to get into the hospital gown. My eyes were locked on a piece of equipment that looked like a big arm without fingers. I wondered if this was the machine he'd use to kill my baby. The thought of that made me cry. I just couldn't hold my tears back. The more I looked around the room, the more the place felt haunted. My heart started pounding really hard and fast, my palms were sweating uncontrollably, and the only thing I was able to do was cry. I felt very scared and lost. I started praying, asking God to help me.

A few minutes later, the doctor walked in again. When he saw me—still fully dressed, tears streaming down my face—he said, "Oh, you're not ready for this. Let me call the father."

I was still frozen at this point; I couldn't seem to move my body or mind. All I was thinking was that if I let this baby grow, it would become just like one of my other babies that I couldn't live without—my babies for whom I would give my life. I was thinking how nice it would be if my son Edriz got to have a brother, a best friend. A lot of ideas were running through my head. But in the end, I knew I couldn't go through with the abortion.

A minute later, Omar walked in with the doctor. He gave me a big smile, and his eyes were glossy and reddish, like he'd been crying. The doctor looked at us both and said, "Well, let's hear the baby's heartbeat." I couldn't believe what was about to happen; I felt equal parts terrified and relieved.

After hearing the heartbeat, I started to cry and smile at the same time. Omar was ecstatic; he was smiling from ear to ear. When we left the office, after collecting our $100 copayment and receiving my prescription for prenatal vitamins, he couldn't stop hugging and kissing me. He kept thanking me for keeping our baby. The drive home felt strange; I knew I'd made the right decision, but now I had different worries. When we got home, I told my mom how I'd ended up not doing it. She too started hugging, kissing and thanking me for keeping it; she said, "You should never reject God's gift." She was as happy as I've ever seen her.

Now, at the age of twenty-six, after filing for divorce three times, I was about to be a mother of four. It was a hard pill to swallow. I had no idea what was going to happen in the future.

I pretty much surrendered to the life I had by keeping the pregnancy. I knew that if I ever left Omar, he would refuse to support me financially. He used to tell me that if I ever left him, he would quit his job just so he wouldn't have to pay me.

Throughout the entire pregnancy, he again called me a penguin. His cussing also never stopped; his favorite thing to say was, "You worthless piece of shit, you cunt!"

He promised he'd quit smoking weed, but of course, that never happened. I felt like I knew him now better than ever. Through the entire pregnancy, I was telling myself that no matter what, I just needed to find a way to somehow escape from him. I was determined to never stop believing that I could do whatever I put my mind to. Throughout everything that had happened, some inner voice of encouragement persisted.

In my fifth month of pregnancy, I was told by my gynecologist that I needed to get a test to take fluid out of my water bag to check my baby for Down Syndrome. To take this test, there was a chance of the amniotic sac getting punctured; my baby could die. I was speechless: all of my other babies had been perfectly healthy and I didn't understand why I needed the test. Though there had been a time I'd been ready to terminate my pregnancy, now I wanted this baby more than anything. If anything ever happened to my baby, I would never forgive myself. I thought maybe God was trying to show me the pain of not having him. I had never been this scared. I started to ask God for forgiveness. I prayed and prayed to keep my baby safe during the test.

After the test, I was told by the doctor and nurses to not do anything but rest in bed, only on my back. I wasn't allowed to move, not even for the bathroom. Omar and my mom would help me use a bedpan for seventy-two hours; otherwise, they said there was a chance that my water could break. So I did whatever I could to keep my baby safe, even though my back felt like it was on a board of needles. I was hot, itchy, heavy and restless.

After seventy-two hours, my doctor called and told me I was now free to walk around and that my baby was healthy as could be. What a relief! I felt like God had forgiven me by letting me know my baby was safe. It was then that I asked him to know the baby's sex. At first I had wanted it to be a surprise, but then I wanted to know. He told me I was having a boy. I was so excited that my son Edriz was going to have a brother and I was going to have two girls and two boys. I was very grateful for what God was blessing me with. A couple of days later, I started to prep my nursery room; I couldn't wait to have my baby boy.

My world felt complete when they put Dylan on my chest on May 29, 1997. I immediately felt like he was my other half (we both are Geminis). I felt amazing holding him, my little soulmate.

Going home with my new baby boy was exciting. I couldn't wait to show him to his siblings and my mom. When we got home, all my babies were running and yelling: "Mom is home, Mom is home!" They all ran toward me, latching onto my legs and asking to see their baby brother. My son Edriz was two years old, Marci was four, and Diana was nine.

The first week I was home with Dylan, things were okay with Omar. But after a couple of weeks of being out of bed and doing things around the house, I felt overwhelmed. It was extremely challenging to manage four children, one of them a newborn. On the other hand, for Omar, the only thing that had changed was that he had more babies to play with and to spoil. He seemed very content with his life. He was fulfilled, thinking that he had the perfect dream life. He had gotten what he wanted, and it didn't matter what I wanted or how I felt.

He may not have physically abused me as much, but instead he would throw and break things around the house more than ever, even around our kids. After twelve years of living with him, I had learned everything I needed to know about him, including how he was as a parent. That was one thing I couldn't ignore. The last thing I wanted was to raise four potheads and beer drinkers with no education, just like their father. My patience with Omar was running out.

Over the next couple of years, I was constantly brainstorming, trying to find ways to get myself out and survive financially, knowing that Omar wouldn't give me a dime. As clean and organized as I kept my home, inside my brain was a complete disaster. Every day I had a new plan.

For the first time, though, I had the beginnings of a viable exit strategy. My best friend Nicole had helped me get my real estate license while I was pregnant with Dylan. Omar hated the idea; when I told him, he had smirked and said, "There's absolutely no way you can do real estate, real estate is not for you."

I replied, "What do you mean, it's not for me? If I can pass my cosmetology board exam on the first try, when my English wasn't even that good? You may doubt me but I know I can do it."

I didn't really have that much confidence in myself, but my best friend Nicole kept encouraging me. She thought I might be really good at it, since I'm a people person. Her belief in me gave me strength. Plus, I was desperate, and didn't really have any other choice. I figured that real estate was the only career in which I could make a lot of money without a degree; I needed to support and maintain my kids' lifestyle, and send money to my family overseas.

When I passed my state board exam, Omar was shocked. He never said much after that, except that he didn't want me to work because of our kids. At the moment, I was fine with that; I wasn't quite ready to take the leap. I guess I was waiting for the right moment. Though our fights were escalating and he was getting more and more verbally abusive, I worried that it was selfish to take my babies away from their father. They got so happy when he came home every day; they would run yelling, "Daddy's home, Daddy's home!" But I also knew deep down that I had to get out.

Now, every time he would recite his favorite refrain—"You worthless piece of shit, go look at yourself in the mirror, you cunt!"—I would reply, "Watch me—I'll show you who's the worthless piece of shit, you asshole!" The older the kids and I got, the more courageous I was becoming. I was no longer afraid of him.

I started learning kickboxing, and I got so good at it that my instructor Steven wanted me to get in the ring and fight. I would always refuse; I'd point at my face and say, "I don't want this face to get ruined."

He would laugh and with a wink, he would say, "That's too bad—I think you would kill it." I was doing so well only because I pictured Omar's face on that punching bag with every punch. This gave me the confidence to fight back. The last time he tried to hit me was when Dylan was two years old; I kneed him in the groin. He was holding my wrists, but my kick was hard enough that he released me. Since then, he never tried to hit me again.

Meanwhile, Omar's drug use was escalating—worse, he started to drug me too.

When I'd decided to not terminate my pregnancy, one of my conditions was for him to stop doing drugs. He had promised over and over that he would never do drugs again if I kept the baby. Once again, I trusted him. I told him that this time around, if I ever saw him on drugs or if he tried to drug me or pressure me, that would be the end of our marriage. He said, "Okay, I promise." But of course, this was a lie.

March 1998 my son Edriz's second birthday with my mom and
my baby girls

When Dylan was about a year old, he took me out to Las Vegas for a weekend getaway. As we were about to leave the hotel room for our dinner reservation, he handed me a drink, and by the time we got to our dinner table I felt full. Although I'd been starving before, I suddenly had no appetite. I ate very little, and by the time we got back into the room, I felt very strange, as if I was about to faint.

As the night went on, I grew extremely weak. At one point I felt I had no strength to even breathe or open my mouth. I felt like I was dying. I whispered to him to call 911, and heard him say, "I can't do that—I'll lose my job if they find out what's in your body."

Instead, he got me a Sprite from the vending machine, saying it would make me feel better. When I didn't improve, he went and got another can. All in all, he got me six cans of Sprite; I'll never forget the sound of the door every time he left the room. After drinking the six cans, I needed to use the bathroom. He helped me to the bathroom and then to bed.

I don't remember anything after that until the next day at 4:00 p.m. I opened my eyes and saw him next to me, dead asleep. I was lying flat on my back, naked; the hotel room ceiling was mirrored, and when I saw myself, I thought I was looking at my ghost. I looked paper-white, almost blending in with the white sheets. I stared at my pale, thin body for a few minutes, trying to remember what had happened to me the night before. My body felt numb, weak, and thirsty. I realized it had to have been the drink he'd handed me right before we left the room—he had drugged me. I felt happy to be alive, like I'd had a narrow escape. But at the same time, I felt manipulated, betrayed and disrespected.

I somehow managed to get up. I didn't say anything; I knew that if I acknowledged it, I'd have to leave him. At that time, I wasn't ready mentally or financially—and my babies were still too young for me to go out and work.

After that, similar things kept happening every couple of months. I suspected that he drugged me often, knowing that I would be less rebellious and more sexually available when I was high. I could never prove it, and he would never admit it, but I knew my body and I kept having the same symptoms again and again—always after I'd taken a drink that he gave me.

Because I knew I wasn't ready yet to leave the marriage, I tried my best to ignore what was happening. But after years of him drugging me regularly, I developed chronic insomnia. Night after night, I would toss and turn, stewing in frustration and anger while he snored right next to me. If I tried to get him to stop snoring, he would get very upset and kick me or hit me, telling me, "Fucking bitch, if you can't sleep, go in the other room."

I had always been very health-conscious and never wanted to take sleeping pills, but at the time I didn't see any other option; I was desperate. I took Advil or Tylenol PM—anywhere from 6–10 pills per night during our last four years of marriage. Sometimes I even took Vicodin. It barely helped, but it was better than nothing. Getting out of bed every morning for my kids' school was the hardest thing to do; I started my days looking and feeling like a zombie. I'll never forget one day I was picking up my daughter Diana from school; at the time, she was 13 years old. When she got in the car, after greeting me, she said "Mom, why do you look like a ghost?"

December 1999 two years before my divorce
during Christmas time

From time to time, I would beg Omar to stop drugging me: what if something happened to me? How would that affect our children? Who would raise them? But he wasn't interested in hearing any of that—he was only interested in drugging me so he could use my body and do what pleased him sexually.

I suffered a great amount of depression due to drugs and insomnia during that time. I'd wake up in the mornings with my eyes and lips puffy, like I'd been punched on the face. I also started to break out on my face and back—something I had never experienced before, not even during my puberty. Even today, I still feel the cumulative result of all the drugs and sleeping pills. I have leaky gut and heartburn, as well as dry mouth, blurred vision and ringing in the ears. I've been seeing a doctor and taking natural medicines, but from my understanding, it will take years and years for these chronic issues to heal.

One night, Omar told me he was going out with a friend from up north. He refused to take me along. I suspected that I knew the reason why; this friend was into snorting drugs. Omar promised me he won't touch drugs, but my intuition wouldn't let go of the idea that something fishy was going on. I decided to go check on him.

I knew that his friend was staying at the Hilton Hotel in Beverly Hills. I got ready, drove to the hotel, and told the front desk clerk that I was here to see Mr. Arun. The clerk called his room; when he told him, "You have a lady by the name of Laila here," I can only imagine Omar's face. When

Omar came down, he was very surprised, and asked me what I was doing there.

I told him, "I wanted to come and see for myself what you guys are up to. I need to see the room to make sure you're not hiding anything from me."

When we walked into the room, I didn't see any drugs, but I could just tell that they were high on cocaine. They were drinking beer. They offered me a drink, and I asked for a bottle of water. After a few minutes, I finished the bottle of water and used the bathroom. I told Omar that we should go home and he didn't hesitate at all.

A strange but pleasant feeling was coming over me: a warm playfulness, combined with an unfamiliar lust for my husband. I told him, "Let's hang out in my car before we get on the road."

He didn't ask why; he just said, "Sure."

I picked up my car from the valet and parked it on a residential street around Sunset Boulevard. I was driving a big Suburban at the time; I told him, "Let's fold down the seats in the back and maybe we can have some fun."

He just looked at me with a smile and said, "Let's do it." We lay down in the back of the car and made out like teenagers.

I wasn't sure what was happening to me. I had never asked Omar to do such a thing before, or wanted to. I'd never felt safe being intimate with him—being playful like that was out of the question. But for some reason, that night I just wanted to be with him.

While we were making out though, I started to smell something bad. At first it seemed like it was coming from somewhere far away. But after a few minutes passed, it was impossible to ignore.

I asked him to turn the light on. When he did, we discovered, to my horror and disgust, that we were sitting in feces—mine, as it turned out. I immediately knew what had happened. I'd heard that when you do cocaine, the first effect is that you lose your appetite, and the second effect is that you lose control of your bowels. I knew he had put something in the water that I'd drank in the room. Funnily enough, when he'd handed me the water, I jokingly said "I hope it's safe" and he'd looked at me with a smirk.

Luckily, I had a gym towel and wipes, and a big bottle of water in the car. We cleaned up as much as we could; I wore his shirt and trashed my clothes. I was furious. I just wanted to kill him. Screaming and crying at the top of my lungs, I kept asking *why, why, why?*

This experience gave me a horrible sense of clarity. This was the final straw. I couldn't let it go.

Back home, the next day, I kept on asking: "Why did I shit myself? Why?" and he would just deny and deny. I asked him to swear on his mother's life, and he did. I knew he was lying, so I kept pressing. I asked him to swear on me, on his kids. He did. I had nothing else left to make him swear on—except for the Quran, which is our holy book.

I had a Quran over our bed on a little shelf. I took the Quran down, brought it to him, and said, "Put your hand and swear to me on this Quran that you did not drug me last night!"

He looked at me with a lost expression. Then, to my own shock, he grabbed the Quran from my hand and drop-kicked it into the next room. It sailed through the double

French doors to our bedroom, over two sets of stairs and finally landed across from the kids' bedrooms with a thud.

I was completely appalled—and, frankly, terrified. This behavior was unheard of for me. It was so important in our culture to respect the Quran: so much so that we aren't even allowed to carry it with one hand. You must carry it with both hands, and before you read it or put it back, you have to kiss it three times. So, drop-kicking it across the length of the house was very, very bad.

I instantly start screaming on the top of my lungs, "MOM!"

My mom anxiously yelled back, "What? What's going on?" I ran crying toward the Quran, my heart racing. I grabbed it tight against my chest and started pacing around the room. I heard my mom walk into the room and repeatedly ask what had happened.

I told her, and then started firing off a series of panicked questions: What was going to happen now? What would the consequences be? Would any of us die? She ignored all of my questions and just started praying, her hands lifted, asking Allah for His forgiveness.

I picked up the phone, called Omar's mom and told her what her son had just done. She immediately hung up the phone and came over. I didn't tell her the real reason behind our fight, just the result. I didn't think she'd believe me anyway.

However, I told my mom everything. I told her about the deal I'd made with Omar, after I decided to keep my baby, that if he ever did drugs or gave me drugs, I'd leave him forever. I told her about the incident in the car the night before. I told her that I was scared for my life and worried that one day this could kill me.

My mom begged me not to make any drastic decisions. She was devastated to hear my story; she cried and cried. But she continued to worry out loud about how my kids and I would survive without any money. She also mentioned my siblings overseas and wondered how they were going to survive. She somehow calmed me down. I told her I'd have to think about it, and that she needed to understand if I ended up staying with him, there was a very real chance that he could kill me. She brushed off my concern and said that he wouldn't do such a thing; she promised to talk to him. But for me, this was something like the final straw: though it would take me a while to actually leave him, seeing him disrespect the Quran like that was something I could never forget or excuse.

At this point, I knew that I had to start getting myself financially established in order to leave this unwanted life without too much financial hardship. It was perfect timing for the real estate market in 2001. I told Nicole about what Omar had done; she didn't seem surprised to hear any of it, except for what the drug had done to me. I told her I was finally ready to start practicing real estate. She encouraged me and offered to set up an interview with her broker, Kim. Prudential Realty was only fifteen minutes from home; I could imagine feeling comfortable working in the same office as her.

Within a week, I signed up for the training class, and within a month I was door knocking. I decided to door knock in my own neighborhood; it was convenient and safe, and I felt it would be easier to attract business among my own neighbors. Omar was not happy about me working or socializing with people from the office, but he was trying to not show it. He knew our relationship was hanging by a thread after his recent behavior, although he kept on denying it.

After I started working, my behavior changed toward him completely. I started to avoid being home with him. If I was, I kept myself busy by doing stuff around the house, avoiding his presence as much as I could. I'd never been this disgusted with him—not even when he locked me out of our apartment balcony while I was three months pregnant on a dark, cold night with just a T-shirt on; not even when he broke my jaw. I couldn't imagine being with him for one more day. How could I ever trust him with my kids? If he could lose so much control as to kick the Quran, what else was he capable of doing?

One day he got home from work in the afternoon, just as I was getting ready to go door knocking. Since I'd always cared about fashion, I was dressed nicely, in a fitted two-piece, olive-green skirt suit, with sheer stockings and heels. In my professional clothes and nametag, I felt pretty and competent. Omar stared me up and down and said, "Why don't you not go today? Let's go do something, just you and I."

I casually said, "I'm sorry, I wish I could, but this is important to me—I have to go." He tried insisting, but I held firm.

After a couple of hours of door knocking, I had to go back home to use the bathroom and check on the kids before going back out. As I walked in through the front door, I heard the kids screaming and crying. Omar was yelling. It sounded insane. When the kids were with me, you'd never hear them scream or cry like that.

I walked into the hallway and stood under the stairs, calling up to see if my kids were okay. All of a sudden, there was a loud crash next to me. It took me a second to realize what had happened: Omar had dropped a glass shower door over my head, from the landing twenty feet above. He had missed me by an inch; the glass had hit the floor and was now shattered into hundreds of pieces. Pieces of shattered glass were everywhere: all over my legs and neck, and wherever my skin was exposed. My beige stockings had lines of blood running through. Even as I stood there bleeding, I could hear him cussing me out, saying, "Come take care of your kids, you cunt! Who do you think would sell their house with a stupid whore like you?"

I yelled back, "I am sooo done with you!"

He just said, "Go ahead and see who's gonna stop you." I'd heard him say this before.

"Fucking douchebag!" I yelled, and then left the house. I drove around for a few minutes to clear my mind, and then went back. My mom was cleaning up the glass and crying; I felt really bad for her in that moment. She was saying how sad she was to see us fight this way and that it was bad for our kids.

I told her, "Mom, this is it, I'm going to see a lawyer tomorrow."

She looked at me with watery eyes and said, "What about your kids? How are you going to survive?"

I said, "I don't know, but I'm going to file for divorce tomorrow."

The next day, I went and hired a divorce attorney. I told him about my situation and got Omar served within a week.

He was losing it. He knew I was serious this time. He immediately started accusing me of having affairs with a friend I'd met in my cycle class, of doing drugs, of not being a good mother. He would not stop calling me, leaving all kinds of nasty inappropriate messages. For over six straight years, every single day, he would call hundreds of times a day, leaving up to thirty messages per day.

He didn't want to move out of the house. I found it hard to kick him out because my kids loved their daddy. They didn't know everything I knew. I decided that, for the kids' sake, he could stay as long as he left his dirty habits outside. When I made this proposal to him, he couldn't believe I was serious. He must have thought that he'd somehow win me back, just like the other three times. He started to be very nice and even playful; I told him he was making a fool out of himself if he thought that I'd change my mind. I reminded him that he'd told me, *Go ahead, cunt, see who's going to stop you.* I said, "Now that it's happening, just be a man!"

That pissed him off, and he started to call me all kinds of names again—the familiar ones, like *fucking whore, you worthless piece of shit.*

Meanwhile, the kids were crying and shouting, "Mom, Dad, please stop, please stop!"

There was so much noise I couldn't take it, so I snapped. I snapped so hard that I opened Omar's closet and started to throw his entire wardrobe downstairs through the bedroom window. I screamed, "Get out, get out now! If you don't, I'm going to call the police right this moment!"

I reached out to my phone to call the police; he smacked it out of my hand and wouldn't give it back. I just kept shouting, "Get out, get out now! If not, then I'll drive to the police station myself!"

Just as I was about to leave, he finally came down, took his keys and left; however, he didn't take any of his clothes. The kids were crying and begging me to let their daddy stay: "Please, Mommy, don't let Daddy go. Please Mommy." It was the hardest thing for me to do to my babies, but I knew in the long run, it was best for all of us.

Divorcing him was hell. Sometimes he made it so hard and difficult that I couldn't take it anymore. I gave in a couple of times, but both times he moved back in, I regretted it instantly and kicked him out again. It was a hell of a rollercoaster for my babies and I.

One day he couldn't get into the house because my mom had the front door lock chain on. After a few minutes of kicking, shaking, yelling and cussing me out, he left. Just as my mom and I were starting to calm down, we heard him coming back, and this time he had a knife. He still couldn't get in because of the chain lock, but we heard him loud and clear.

I stayed quiet and told my mom, "It's best if he thinks I'm not home." I didn't know what to expect, based on how much he had hurt me physically and mentally in the past; I wouldn't have been surprised if he'd tried to kill me. But I was ready. I no longer feared him; if anything, I wanted him to try to hurt me so that maybe I could hurt him back in self-defense. By now, I'd been doing kickboxing for six years; with my experience, I was ready!

He tried very hard in court to get my babies away from me, but I fought and fought. He didn't think I could last financially since the lawyer fees kept piling up, but he had no idea how much money I was making in real estate. I had started to find clients and was doing very well.

One night my mom and I were watching TV, and my mom, as always, was trying to brainwash me to get back together with Omar. She would say things like, "The kids are missing having their dad around, and you'll never make it financially." She always cried for me, seeing the blisters on my toes from door knocking six days a week. I was always on the go, with barely any time to eat. I was working full-time while taking care of my four kids, not to mention my mom with all of her doctor's appointments; I was financially responsible for eighteen people. It was a lot of pressure.

Hearing all of my mom's negativity and doubts made me very upset. I told her to stop and have some faith in me. I promised her that her kids and grandkids would never starve or be homeless as long as I was around.

During our conversation, my phone rang. It was Omar. I told my mom, and she said, "Aww, how sad, he's probably missing his life with you and the kids. Why don't you answer?"

I don't know why I even listened to her, but I did. The second I answered "Hello," I heard him telling me, "You took my boys away from me, I wanted to play ball with them and you took them away from me."

When I heard the pain in his voice, I just cried for him. I forgot about everything else except how much he was hurting. All I said to him was that he'd done it to himself. I knew that if I gave him one more chance, things would never be the same.

I barely slept that night, thinking of what he'd said about playing ball with my boys and the importance of them having a father. The next morning at 9:00 a.m., I called him and said, "Look, I've been thinking all night about what you said last night. What if we try one more time, but this time it'll be different. You won't move back in, but you can come hang out with us after work and spend your days off with the kids."

Basically, I was proposing that we live a normal life, except that he couldn't sleep in the same house or want to be with me physically. I told him that we'd never had a chance to get to know each other due to our arranged marriage, so I suggested that we try dating. He agreed to everything.

Later that afternoon, I got home from work around 5:00 p.m. The second I stepped into the house, I heard Omar's voice with the kids. I instantly felt the rush of hot blood through my entire body, followed by the chills. I told myself, "Oh my god, what did I do?"

I immediately regretted it. But now what? I could hear him telling the kids to "come help him hang Daddy's shirt." I said to myself: hanging his shirt? The deal was for him not to move in and for us to take it slow and get to know one another. Had he broken his word already?

On his first night back, I kept myself busy with laundry; the last thing I wanted to do was sleep next to him. Just hearing his voice was giving me goosebumps. Around 11:00 p.m., as I was folding the laundry, he started asking me when I was going to come to bed. I told him that I was busy and wouldn't be in until later. I said, "I hope you're not expecting anything from me."

He assured me he wasn't expecting anything and that he was just asking to see if I'd want to have a cigarette with him.

I asked him, "Since when do you smoke?" He knew I had smoked sometimes, here and there. I told him I didn't have any cigarettes on me and I didn't care to smoke.

He had told me that he had some. I asked, "Since when do you carry a pack?"

He claimed it was his uncle Zamir's. He lit the cigarette for me, then handed it to me; we both smoked one in the garage.

Omar again asked if I was ready for bed. I said, "Not yet—just go to sleep and I'll get in once I'm done with my laundry."

But he wouldn't take no for an answer. He kept going back and forth from upstairs to downstairs, slamming and banging doors, and trying really hard to wake the kids up so he could ruin my night, all because I was ignoring him. I finally had to give in. My mom told me, "Please go to bed, it's too late for the kids to wake up with all these loud noises, it'll scare them."

It was now past 1:00 am. When I went to bed, he was waiting for me. The second I got to bed, he reached out to me and tried to grab me. I tried so hard to push him away, telling him that if he tried anything it would be over and that he was breaking his promise. But he didn't care. No matter how much I resisted, he forced himself on me.

Afterwards, falling asleep was out of the question. My brain was filled with all kinds of thoughts. I wanted to kill him. I wanted to do anything to be away from him, but then what would happen with my babies? The sun was now up but I didn't want to get up and face reality.

I couldn't even tell my mom, because culturally there are some things that just can't be spoken of. Also, she would never understand the word 'rape'; to her, if husbands forcefully sleep with their wife, it isn't considered rape.

I was very disappointed with myself, after everything I'd been through. Getting him out of the house was one of the hardest things I'd ever done; it had taken enormous courage. But once again, he had fooled me. I felt stupid and naïve that I'd believed him again. I felt stuck and sick to my stomach knowing how happy my babies were that their dad was back. I just couldn't put them through another horrible experience by having him out again. I basically had to ignore the fact that he did not keep his promise.

I felt like a cigarette might help calm me down, remembering that he'd left the pack of cigarettes on top of the garage refrigerator the night before. He'd said he would leave them there in case I wanted more. Now that I thought about it, the whole thing seemed off: he used to beat me up for occasionally smoking with his younger siblings, and now he was offering me a pack?

I found the pack of cigarettes and pulled a cigarette out. I noticed that the cigarette was a strange yellowish-brown color, as if it had gotten wet and then dried out. I couldn't figure out why it looked like that. When I tried to light the cigarette, it almost didn't light; I had to light it several times until I was finally able to inhale some smoke. It instantly made me cough, but besides that, it tasted very strange: a gasoline-like taste that is hard to describe.

I started to investigate the pack inside and out. Nowhere on the pack felt wet, but the few cigarettes were all stained with long yellow lines. I was very curious. I tried to light another cigarette and it did the same thing. I was very confused. I then grabbed a third one; this time I turned the cigarette upside down to see if there was something wrong with the tobacco. I noticed what looked like little tiny pieces of clear glass mixed in with the tobacco.

I took one of the tiny little pieces of glass with the tip of my pinky finger nail. I put it in my mouth. At this point my heart was racing; I knew that he had mixed the tobacco with something, to try and drug me. The taste of that tiny clear object was the worst thing I'd ever tasted—like gasoline or some sort of burned rubber. I immediately started retching and puked my guts out right there in the garage. As the spasms subsided, I was speechless, wondering how he could do this to me after everything.

I ran quickly inside the house and told my mom what he had done. I didn't think she would believe me; in the past, when I used to tell her, she would just brush it off. However, this time around, I think she could see it on my face, since it was obvious I'd just been puking my brains out. She was curious too as to what it was, so she also put a tiny piece in her mouth. Immediately, she ran for the bathroom. I thought to myself, *At least she believes me now.*

Afterwards, she freaked out and begged me to go to the hospital. I looked at her, laughing. "Do you believe me now?

I've been trying to tell you for years that he was trying to kill me by constantly drugging me."

I told my mom that there was no way we could confront him; if we did, that would mean I'd have to kick him out again. However, I still wanted to know what he had mixed into the cigarettes. I thought I'd take it to my lawyer. He was an older man in his sixties, with older kids. He always tried to talk me out of divorce, since I had four young kids and was still very young myself with unreliable income. He looked at the cigarettes and then shook his head. "That's crystal meth," he said.

I wasn't surprised, for obvious reasons. I told him to keep the cigarette in my file as evidence. "In case something happens to me," I said, "just know that he's my murderer." Funnily enough, after that, my lawyer never again asked me to try to work on my marriage.

After that, I avoided being home whenever Omar was home, and slept in my boys' bedroom. When it became obvious that I was ignoring him, it made him go crazy. He would brainwash our kids, making up stories about why I'd tried to leave him. Every time he would say something bad about me, my kids would come to me and ask if it was true. I just told him, "You can tell them whatever you want. When they're older, they'll know the truth." It was heartbreaking to see him using them like this. The last thing I ever wanted was to see them suffer.

One day, a couple of weeks after he'd moved back in, he came to my room with our oldest daughter Diana, who was fifteen at the time. While I was changing out of my work clothes, he said, "Why don't you tell her?"

I asked, "What do you mean, tell her what?"

He said, "You know what I'm talking about. Just spit it out, tell her why you want a divorce from me."

I told him again, "I have no idea what you're talking about." I looked at my daughter and said, "You'll know the truth on your own."

He said, "Let me tell you then, why she wants a divorce. It's because she likes girls. It's important that you know your mother is now a lesbian and she fucks girls."

Diana looked at me, amazed, her big brown eyes round with disbelief. It was obvious that she wasn't buying it and that she just felt bad for me.

I asked Diana to leave the room and to shut the door so I could talk to Omar. I told him how much he disgusted me. I confronted him about trying to drug me again, and of course, as usual, he denied it. I replied and said, "Sure, the pack is with my lawyer so we'll see in court." I finished getting dressed and left the room.

I went downstairs and told my daughter Diana that what he'd said was all a lie. I told her that what he'd just done was way out of line, and that there was no way I could put up with this for the rest of my life. Diana looked at me with teary eyes and didn't say anything; I gave her a tight hug and assured her that our life would be much better without him. At that moment, I realized that I was hurting my kids even more than ever if I stayed with him.

I left the house and didn't come home until the next day around 5:00 p.m. I told my mom my whereabouts—I was at my friend Safia's—but made her promise not to tell Omar. I told her I was leaving him for the last time. She too was in disbelief about his behavior and didn't try to stop me. When I got home the next day, I didn't expect him to be home.

But apparently, he'd left work early so he could catch me. As soon as I saw his car in the driveway, my heart dropped. I knew that he'd go crazy knowing I was just now getting home from last night.

I didn't know what to expect; I just knew it wasn't going to be good. I found him in the family room. It looked like he also had just gotten home from work; he was still in his suit. The first thing that came out of his mouth when he saw me was, "Did you fuck someone?"

The kids were right there. I responded by saying, "Yes, I did, and it's none of your business."

He came closer to me, holding a big glass of ice water. My heart was pounding. Although I was playing it tough, inside I was terrified. I had never talked to him like that before.

For a second, I thought he was going to kill me as he was walking toward me. Chewing his lower lip, a look of menace in his green eyes: he looked like a cobra that was about to infect me with his poison. He threw the glass of ice water at me, and the glass fell to the ground and shattered. The kids were crying, my mom was trying to ask questions about what happened, and I just lost it. I was so sick and tired of him, more so than ever. I knew if I stayed, his anger would progress and only God knows what he'd do.

I yelled, "It's finally over, Omar, do you hear me? It's over, this is it!"

I walked toward the garage, and he followed me. We were both shouting. The kids seemed scared; they were crying, and my mom was trying to calm them down. Right before I shut the car door, I yelled out, "I'll see you in court!"

He said, "Go ahead and see who'll stop you this time."

I just laughed and said, "Okay, we'll see."

The next day, I went to my lawyer's office told him to continue with the filing. This time around, my lawyer didn't hesitate; he immediately said, "No problem."

Getting Omar out of the house for the second time wasn't any easier than the first time, but I knew I had no choice, and this time I succeeded. The entire time, I was constantly reminding myself to not ever let him fool me again. Doing that allowed me to keep my head straight and not get sidetracked by his manipulative behavior.

Within months, Omar went to Pakistan for a couple of weeks and came back with pictures of a Nikah (marriage) ceremony, showing him being wed to a 15-year-old girl. This was perfectly legal in Pakistan, for him to marry a minor despite being already married.

Somehow, he thought this would make me take him back—but of course, it had the opposite effect. It made me more anxious than ever to get him out of our lives. He begged and cried and would send family members to talk me out of the divorce. However, I was clearly done with him this time. If he was serious about his family, he would have worked on changing himself, rather than going and marrying an innocent young girl and taking her virginity, as if this would make me come back!

A few weeks prior to her arrival to the US, Omar called to ask me if I would be interested in listing a property he'd bought for investment. I didn't want to turn a listing down, so I took the property information from him, prepped a comparable market analysis, and scheduled to meet him at his investment property the next day. As soon as I walked in, he looked at me from head to toe, smiled and said, "I just wanted to talk to you before I sign anything. The girl I did the Nikah ceremony with has all her paperwork done and ready—she's just waiting for me to get her ticket to fly out here. But I can easily not do that if you want to give me one more chance."

I simply couldn't believe what he was telling me. I just stared at him, shocked. I replied, "You had sixteen years of chances," and walked out.

A couple of days later, he listed the property with my ex-real estate partner, just to irritate me. I was in disbelief: how could a father refuse to help out the mother of his four kids, just out of spite? After all, he wasn't providing any financial support as far as child support or alimony—the least he could do would be to give me his business.

In case you're wondering why he wasn't paying child support: the judge had in fact ordered him to pay $4,900.00 per month for child support and alimony, based on his average monthly income (which didn't include his bonuses). I only received it once. During that month, he harassed me constantly: I received incessant calls claiming that I was taking his money and spending it on other men, that I was a whore, and worse. It was hard enough for me to work seven days a week, with no day off, while taking care of my babies at the same time; I had no energy to respond to his harassment.

These calls were endless, and they were hurting my business: as a real estate agent, I couldn't afford to miss any important calls, and his incessant harassment made it difficult to do my job. Plus, I was doing so well in my business that I knew I could cover my expenses without his contribution. I liked the idea of being totally free from him, financially as well as physically. So I told my lawyer to drop the child support and alimony to zero.

As for custody, that broke down as well. During the first year after I filed for divorce, my kids missed twenty-six days of school, because when Omar had them, he would pick them up early or drop them off late—or sometimes not bring them to school at all. At one point, I got called in for a meeting with their teachers because they were missing so much school. I was shocked: I'd had no idea he was doing this. I knew that if they missed more school, child services could be called and they could be taken away from me. That wasn't something I was willing to risk. I explained the situation to their teachers, and they understood. But this situation motivated me to fight even harder in the divorce.

He did everything in his power every single day for the next six years to call me. At times there would be over 150 disgusting voicemails—not just about me but also my parents, siblings and friends. He tried to make every day of my life miserable.

After his new bride arrived in the US, she started to join him on the absurd, nasty voicemails. It seemed like he had found his perfect match; her mouth was even dirtier than his. But I didn't blame her. Growing up in a country that had been at war for over forty years, with no access to education and hardly any jobs, you learn to survive somehow, even if you have to do dirty to people. She was just another victim of an arranged marriage. Her parents, by marrying their 15-year-old daughter to a 48-year-old man, had helped themselves by gaining the financial support of their new son-in-law.

But one unexpected benefit of the new wife's arrival was that Omar stopped fighting for the kids after that, because she didn't want them around. This worked in my favor, since I never liked my kids to be around him or anyone else but me and my mom (who was living with me at the time). After that, he rarely saw them. We occasionally saw him at family functions, such as cousins' weddings, engagement parties, and things like that. Other than that, he never made any effort to see the kids, not even on their birthdays or during the holidays. He didn't even send birthday cards. There were times he didn't see them for years. Today, I refer to him as their 'sperm donor'.

When I became a single parent, it was important to me to raise my kids with structure and consequences—the kind that had been almost impossible to enforce when Omar was around. I established some important rules that were not to be broken. I had a piece of paper on the fridge with all their names on it; whenever they said or did something bad, like calling each other names, I would note it on the paper and there would be consequences.

I gave them weekly allowances based on their ages: for example, if they were six years old, I gave them six dollars a week. Each mark against their behavior, written on the refrigerator sheet, would cost them a dollar. After all was said and done, they were allowed to spend half of their remaining allowance on sweets or ice cream; the other half they had to save. Through this practice, I tried to teach them the value of a dollar.

I also held family meetings once a month on Sundays. If they were behaving badly, the family meetings became more frequent. Our family meetings took place in their game room; I would sit them all down on the couch and I would sit right across from them with a notepad and the sheet from the fridge with their names on it. I'd go over their behavior, and they were not allowed to talk or say something unless they raised their hand, just like a classroom.

It took time to build and enforce this kind of structure, since Omar had always let them do whatever they wanted. But over time, it began to stick, and I saw them thrive in school and grow into the wonderful people they are today.

*June 2001 First family picture after my fourth
time filing for divorce*

In the meantime, I focused single-mindedly on my career. I was very determined to show Omar, and anyone else who'd ever doubted me, that I wasn't a "worthless piece of shit"; if anything, I could provide a better life for myself and my babies, along with my family in Pakistan, than he could.

I built a successful business. My first year, I made over $120,000. My second year, I doubled that; and the following year, I doubled my income again. I also got into investments in real estate. By the time I was thirty-four years old, I was making over half a million dollars per year and owned seven investment properties.

The feeling of being independent and successfully taking care of all my loved ones was priceless. For the first time in my life, I was enjoying myself to the fullest. I made my own decisions, without being forced to do anything; I felt free and worthy. I didn't mind working as hard as I did; I was unstoppable. Going door knocking every day, whether it rained or shined, was better than being married to Omar. My life felt complete.

I was not interested in dating until about three years after my divorce in 2004. I was at a printing shop to pick up my fliers to door knock. As I left the printing shop, walking toward my car, I heard a man calling me: "Miss, miss, I'm sorry to bother you—my name is Leon. I couldn't help but hear that you're a real estate agent?"

I replied, "Yes, I am." He asked if I wouldn't mind checking out a property for him down the street to see if the owners might be interested in selling. I agreed; he shared the property's address, we exchanged phone numbers, and I told him I'd call him once I got some information.

Though he didn't end up buying that house, we stayed in touch and became friends. Every once in a while, I would show properties to him and his wife, Lisa, and occasionally we would meet for lunch. Leon seemed very curious about my single life and tried for a couple of years to set me up with one of his doctor friends. At that time, I was not interested in being in a relationship.

Leon reached out one day and told me he had a friend who was looking to buy a house and that he had referred him to me. He had sent me referrals in the past, so I thanked him and thought nothing of it. The next day, I called Leon's friend and scheduled to show him properties based on his criteria. After a couple of showings, the client sent me two dozen red roses with a note asking me out to dinner.

The first thing I did was to call Leon and tell him about the roses. I needed to know who this guy really was. He laughed and said, "This is the friend I've been trying to set you up with."

At first, I was not interested in replying to the client's note. But when I went home that day, I told my mom about this Indian doctor client of mine, how he'd sent me flowers and asked me on a date. I told her I wasn't interested, that I wasn't ready to be in a relationship.

My mom had other ideas. She went on and on, telling me about the importance of having a role model and father figure in my kids' life. She pointed out that he had a good profession and could maybe even help my kids be inspired to become doctors someday. I thought about what my mom said for a couple of days, and it kind of made sense; I decided to at least consider it, although I wasn't attracted to him at all—he was fourteen years older than me and I thought he looked like an old uncle. I was living my life for my kids; my kids were my heart and soul, and I would do anything to make sure they had a good life.

I decided to finally respond after a couple of days to his note. I just asked, "What time?"

He quickly replied and said, "How about I pick you up around 7:00 p.m.?"

Just like that, this man came into my life. I ended up staying with him for ten years.

On our first date, he told me that he had been legally separated for two years now and that his divorce would be filed soon. I believed him. The first two years of dating him were nice; he was absent a lot, but I didn't mind that, since I was very busy myself with work and my kids. When we were together, he was a real gentleman; he treated me like a queen. Especially after my experience with Omar, he seemed too good to be true.

After a couple of years, though, I started to question his story about his divorce. He had told me on our first date that his divorce shouldn't take more than two years to be finalized. But as time went by, my questions multiplied. The answer was always the same: "It's in process."

Over the next few years, I broke up with him three times. But each time, he persistently called, texted and sent gifts and flowers; he pleaded, telling me how he couldn't see his life without me and promising that he was getting his divorce as soon as his court case got settled (he had a hospital suing him for some kind of negligence).

Finally, I realized that I was being manipulated and used. Despite his promises, he had no intention of following through on his divorce. He may not have done drugs or physically abused me, but it had been another bad relationship filled with nothing but lies and manipulation. Knowing that I deserved better, I ended the relationship. He never stopped pursuing me, but I knew I could never trust him again.

When I look back on that relationship now, I think of how easy it is to stay caught in a cycle of abuse and bad relationships when that's all you've ever known. I had never had a healthy, consensual relationship with a man before; I hadn't yet fully learned to trust my own instincts or ask for what I needed.

My experience with Omar, and with my subsequent partner, had taught me to be suspicious and doubtful, never fully trusting a man or letting him into my heart. I learned to be free with my love and feelings. I learned not to have my guard up. It took me a long time to learn how to be in a healthy relationship—but today I'm the happiest woman.

I am also happy to report that my children are doing well. My eldest daughter, Diana, followed my path in real estate. After five years in the field, she met her husband and started a family. I am now a grandmother to her sons. My other daughter, Marci, received her bachelors in Business Law and is currently following a path to obtain her Masters in Law. My son, Edriz, is a successful business owner and also self-taught graphic and fashion designer. My youngest son, Dylan, started his career in commercial real estate, before joining a tech startup company and eventually leaving to pursue his own path in entrepreneurship.

In 2018, I decided to change my career to fashion—long a passion of mine—with a particular goal in mind. I wanted to do something that I thoroughly loved and enjoyed. Growing up, fashion always played a huge role in my life: it provided a form of escape for me. Often, when I tried clothes on, it gave me a sense of freedom and power. I enjoy playing dress-up and mixing and matching shoes and accessories. My daughters and I would call it "Laila's fashion show"; till this day, I still do it. I finally decided to attend FCI fashion school in Los Angeles so I could learn to create and design timeless evening gowns as well as everyday wear—not only to fulfill my passion and desire for fashion, but to also help my non-profit organization.

Conclusion

August 2022 me with my children today

September 2006 in Laguna Beach with my biological brothers and sister.

Epilogue

My story may be deeply personal and specific, but its broader outline is sadly not uncommon. The toxic culture that leads to forced arranged marriages—the patriarchal value of men over women, and the treatment of women and girls as property—has been around for centuries and centuries, especially in the Middle East.

By some measures, forced marriage has become less and less prevalent over time. Unfortunately, with the Taliban back in power in Afghanistan, it's like we've turned the clock back one hundred years. Women's rights have regressed steeply, even in cities. Education often played a huge role in women's ability to advocate for themselves, but access to schooling has always been distributed unevenly—in rural areas, schools are not as accessible due to poverty, and this situation is much worse under the Taliban.

That doesn't mean that modern families with education don't practice forced arrange marriages; as in my own family, if the parents felt like the guy comes from a good family, with a well-known name, they often believe they know what's best for their daughters and arrange a marriage—whether the girl is happy or not.

Throughout the world, little girls are being taking away from their parents—or sometimes given away or sold by parents who can't afford to feed them. We need to help them to escape to a safe home and gain access to education.

Though this problem is widespread in Middle Eastern countries, it's not inherently an Islamic issue. People have been wrongfully taught that the Quran sanctions forced marriage, but in reality that's not the case. In the Quran, Allah speaks of husband and wife with equality and respect, and advises that they obey each other[4]. However, this passage has been interpreted as favoring men. Men think that once they get married, their wife becomes their personal property. This belief comes from centuries of patriarchal laws and traditions; it doesn't come from Allah.

The good news is that this means it can be changed. We can best honor our religion and honor God by respecting all human life equally. So many women and girls are suffering needlessly at this very moment. The culture of forced arranged marriage needs to be broken, for their sake and for the children of the future.

I want to be clear that my story isn't about blaming my parents for how they raised me or arranged my marriage. It's about using my story to illuminate larger cultural patterns. This is an ongoing matter that many parents in the Middle

---

[4] One relevant quotation: "O believers! It is not permissible for you to inherit women against their will or mistreat them to make them return some of the dowry as a ransom for divorce—unless they are found guilty of adultery. If you happen to dislike them, you may hate something which Allah turns into a great blessing." Quran 4:19

East still practice as the norm. It goes back generations. Sons watched their mothers being abused by their fathers, and daughters watched their mothers accepting it without a question asked. For those reasons, the trend of forced and abused marriages has gone on and on for centuries.

Growing up, I had a lot of resentment toward my parents, but as I grew into adulthood, I started to understand why they made the decisions they did. Although we lived in Europe, they were operating by the laws of a culture that told them they had ownership over their children and could make choices for them.

Yes, it's true that due to my parents' decision, so many of my dreams died, and I'll have to live for the rest of my life wondering *what if?* What if I had been allowed to choose my own partner, or choose to remain unmarried? What if I had been able to finish my schooling at my own pace and pursue the career I wanted? I'll never know the answers to these questions.

Still, I now truly believe that my parents are not to be blamed for their actions—whether it was my arranged marriage or my mother allowing my father to separate our family or my stepmom treating us the way she did. All of this has a lot to do with culture and tradition, and in some cases, education. It also has to do with trauma: we unconsciously repeat the destructive patterns of our own childhoods until we learn that something else is possible. I have learned to forgive my family and love them all unconditionally.

Rather than mourning the dreams that were lost, I want to accept the life I have and find meaning in what I've been through. I am now certain that my purpose is to be a voice for those who are suffering at this very moment from a forced arranged marriage or stuck in a cycle of abuse. My past made me who I am today, and while I wouldn't wish what I've been through on anyone, I am proud of who I've become as a result.

I like to believe we all are here for a reason and that all of our experiences can contribute to our life's purpose. Maybe my dreams had to die so that I could educate my children how to be stronger humans and how to find their own purpose. I raised my kids to know their worth, to never take life for granted, to know there's more to life than just growing up and getting married. I raised them to make the most of any experience. I tried to give them the best of Middle Eastern and Western cultures.

As an Afghan woman, I'm proud of my culture: there's so much beauty in it, such as our hospitality—we go above and beyond for our guests. It's precisely because I love my culture that I want to fix its more toxic elements—to break the custom of forced arranged marriage.

I also find meaning in my experience through the knowledge that perhaps I can help other women in situations like what I went through. Looking back, there were several factors that enabled me to escape from my abusive marriage after sixteen years. One was daily exercise. I enjoyed going to the gym or working out at home; it gave me a tremendous amount of relief and helped me access endorphins that allowed me to have a smile on my face for my kids and to get through the day. Eventually, it also gave me a sense of my own strength and power, and helped me stand up to my husband.

Watching Oprah's show encouraged and inspired me to not fall for false promises and to give up on thinking I could change my partner for the better. Today, with the existence of the Internet, similarly lifesaving information and motivation is available at the tips of your fingers. I was also fortunate to have great friends who helped me to believe in myself and know that I was good enough to do whatever I chose to do. This gave me the confidence to become independent in all areas in my life.

If you are in an abusive relationship, I hope that my story has given you some hope and provided you with some tools to advocate for yourself. You may feel alone, but you are not alone.

If I could give advice to my younger self, or those in a similar situation, it would be this: don't be ashamed or too shy to stick up for yourself. Don't hold back your eagerness or assertiveness; these are important parts of who you are. Don't let anybody lay hands on you without your consent. Your body is your own. Seek help without fear; there is no shame in sharing your pain and suffering with people who might be able to help you. Above all, avoid hurting yourself or trying to take away your own life. Your life is precious, and you are worth it. If you can, find a way to go to school; no matter what, try to educate yourself in any way possible. You deserve better and you can do anything you want. Lastly, trust your intuition: when you know, you know.

It is my hope that telling my story will not only touch the hearts and minds of readers, but also contribute to substantial material change. All proceeds of this book will go to help women and girls in forced marriages. If you have been touched by my story, I encourage you to donate to my non-profit 'IWANTFREEDOM.NGO' and, whether or not you can donate, to spread the word about this issue and help amplify the voices of abused women and girls.

Fathers and mothers, sisters and brothers, daughters and sons, I need you: without your help, this is just an empty dream. Together, we can save some of these innocent young girls and women, who in some cases are as young as five years old. Without your help, I can't bring them to safety and provide them with the education and life lessons that will allow them to reach a brighter future. This is an issue that affects millions of women all over the world, including here in the US; we are all human, and together we can make a change.